OPEN YOUR HEART
AND SAY "AHHH"

STORIES AND OBSERVATIONS FROM A
FRIZZY-HAIRED THERAPIST

by

DR. SUSAN POMERANZ

ACKNOWLEDGMENTS

I want to thank the Academy...Oh...wrong speech.

I want to thank Norman Thalheimer—the love of my life. His contribution to this book was enormous. In all honesty, this truly was a collaborative effort. Not only is he really funny, creative and inspiring, but he's off the charts brilliant. So pretty much any word over three syllables and a lot of the good jokes came from him.

My deepest appreciation to my editor and friend, Rick Schultz. He was invaluable to me. He taught me the stuff I never learned in school because I was too busy trying to figure out all the people in my classes, like the shop teacher with three fingers and the girl with the beehive and hickey on her neck. He also took great care to make sure words like "heinie" and "bubkis" were spelled consistently throughout.

I also want to thank my parents, Mel and Bonnie, and my brother, David Pomeranz. They are the sweetest souls in the land and the reason for all the love and fun in my heart.

Thank you to Steve Horwitch, Peter Ulikhanov, Jeff San Marchi, Kelly Yaegermann, Nicky Pomeranz, Linda Orber, Kitty Thalheimer, Althea Schwartz, Zack Schwartz, Victoria Larimore, Janice Hubbard, J.D. and Sheridanne, and to all my beautiful clients who have graced my life.

MY GRATITUDE COULD FILL THE SKY.

This is dedicated to the one I love

CONTENTS

INTRODUCTION

I see crazy people. All day long. Crazy, interesting, wonderful people. My name is Susan Pomeranz. I'm a marriage and family therapist with over twenty years of private practice in Los Angeles (where everyone is arguably "crazy," so business is very good), and I have a piece of advice for you, even if you don't live in LA: Open Your Heart and Say "AHHH."

The title, *Open Your Heart and Say "AHHH,"* is a play on words, but you've probably already figured that out. Its pages are bursting with the wonderful, crazy people I learn from every day. These people deal in unique ways with life, sex, money, food, drugs, relationships, bad hair days, and perhaps most depressingly, Comedy Traffic School, the most unfunny place in this or any universe.

In these pages, you'll meet the Ugliest Woman on Earth (she decided it was so, and it was so); a teenager who came to grips with his sexuality while seated in my office, stroking a stuffed cat; a woman gathering tremendous courage as she goes blind; people with insane hair (I don't like to brag...); and a hundred more intrepid and, uh, crazy people. The stories are brief, funny, sad, helpful, and human. At the end of each story, there are exercises that might help you resolve similar issues, because human is as human does.

Let me tell you a bit more about myself. It will save you

time flipping back and forth, looking at the picture and reading that little blurb at the back of the book. Officially, I started practicing therapy right after I cut my long hippie hair (the Jewish version of the Cher, "I Got You Babe"-years) and got my first Donna Summers disco perm.

I've been in the trenches working with people all through the experimental hair-dye years of the '80's and '90's, right into the sleek, glossy, stick-straight millennial years. Like some of you, I've purchased almost every hair product known to (wo)man. I now have enough gel and "moisture" to lubricate 106 motorcycles, 97 diesel trucks, the Tin Man, and to help 86 women through peri-menopause.

By far, the straight hair period was the toughest on me. Besides the extra six hours a day it took me to get everything to lay straight, by the time I put my 36-lb ionic hair dryer away and opened the door to my car (caution: don't drink and dry), my hair was back to its original form, á la Barbara Streisand in "The Main Event"—or, for those of you who don't remember, think: Don King or Carrot Top.

I'm still at it, both the therapy and the hair, and as I write this, the work is still deeply joyful and the hair, well, that's a more cleaned up layered version back to early Cher. I must admit I've learned a lot from my hair. I've finally learned just to let it be. I've learned to bring out its true nature. I've learned to accept it, nourish it, transcend it and ultimately get into the miracle of life—which is the very essence of what the healing process should be.

Helping people create joyful, sane, and loving lives is my passion. I wrote *Open Your Heart and Say "AHHH"* in this spirit. It's designed to lift the reader to a new place of thinking and being. My intent is to foster humor, compassion, contribution and endless possibilities. It is created to elevate and motivate the heart and soul into action.

I purposely kept the chapters in this book short--little

bite-size pieces to read and digest at your leisure and, I hope, your pleasure. Since learning should be experiential and fun, my goal was to make this information accessible, practical, and as useful as possible.

Feel free to read this book in any way you'd like. Peruse the table of contents. Perhaps the titles will guide you toward what feels right; or, if you're like me, just randomly open the book and start reading. Today I opened it to the chapter "On Sex." But, sadly, my boyfriend opened his copy up to "The Power of No." Go figure.

Please join me in putting the laughter, magic and passion back into our days. All we need to do is open our hearts and say "AHHH."

PART I.
ON AND BEYOND
THE COUCH

ON SEX

It was a steamy, hot, sweaty summer day. The UPS man's body was drenched and glistening with moisture as he gripped the big hard package and rang her door bell. She was scantily clad as she opened her door. She was panting and her breasts were heaving because she was feeling moist and hot. As she opened the door and saw him, she felt a stirring in her loins and her whole body ached with excitement and hunger. Rod, that's his name, now had his own big hard package for her (that makes two). Their eyes met and their gaze said everything. After a silence that felt like an eternity, she finally said, "I'm so hot and throbby, and I was just about to take a shower. Would you like to join me?" He quickly dropped one of his packages...

Okay, that was totally fun. Do I have your attention? Now let's talk about sex. As a culture we are obsessed with it. Just flip through any magazine at your local book store or checkout stand. You'll see: Are you hot enough? Sexy enough? Is your penis big enough? Hard enough? Are your breasts perky and pouty? Do they point upwards toward Canada or 17-degrees South of Mexico? Do you talk to your lover in bed and yell things like, "You're the King!" (Be careful of that one--you might call in the neighbors' dog.) A quick aside: I wonder if atheists ever yell "Oh, God!" in the throws of passion. I actually

3

had a neighbor who nightly used to yell "No! No! No! No!" I could never figure it out. I just hope there was some-body else in there with him.

No, really. Have you ever read "Cosmo" or "Glamour" or other estrogen magazines where they have all these groundbreaking statistics, like 81% of all couples use some kind of food item as part of their love making? Let's address this one. First of all, if you have any tendencies toward anorexia, food is definitely out. Also, unless you are first dating or high on crack in some mirrored hotel room somewhere, or you don't have to wash your own sheets the next day, how many women do you think are running to the cupboard for the Welch's' Grape Jelly? And really, why waste good chocolate fudge sauce? After all, you're so looking forward to eating it when everyone finally leaves the house.

Come on, where do they get this stuff anyway? And the sex quizzes? "Do you like it on a chair? Do you like it in the air?" (Sounds like Dr. Seuss). "Do you use a dia-phragm?" "Do you fill it with some jam?" (Okay, one more.) "Do you scream and say, Oh Lord, while you're humping in a Ford?" You try some.

Also, apparently there are now 36 G spots (not counting Pluto). Actually, that's 35 more than I knew about.

Besides fostering absurd comparisons and oodles of self doubt, it's all about mechanics. Have we forgotten about truly loving each other? We still look outside of ourselves to see what is "normal" or how we should be, versus looking inside for what feels right. It doesn't matter if you make love constantly or only in months that end in *anuary*, or haven't had sex since Alaska and Hawaii were admitted to the Union. This is not the issue.

What matters is what's right for you. Are you able to fully express your heart and share the deepest parts of

4

yourself? Is there a reciprocity to your loving that grows and evolves as you do?

Many couples come into my office with sexual issues. "She's too tired/ He's too mired/ He's not exciting/ She's not inviting." But isn't sex just a barometer for what's going on anyway? I often tell couples to stop having sex. Just stop. Game over. It's no longer about orgasm and coming and going. Instead, it's about all the ways we can be pleasuring and loving and intimate with each other. It's amazing the levels of connection and tenderness and playfulness people find when they do this. Sometimes they discover that sex can actually be a deflection from real intimacy.

Love yourself and each other. I can't say this enough. Forget about how old you are or what you weigh or if you're round or boney or your skin is not age 25. Screw it! I had an interesting experience many years ago. You know how during sex you check yourself out so you look a certain way? Totally out of present time, obsessed with thoughts of fat and how you look and afraid that if you got on top, your sagging flesh might hit your loved one in the head and possibly knock them out?

Well, I got to experience the other side. I had a partner who felt overweight and was completely self-conscious and self-absorbed (even more than I was; life is so funny). It was a total drag. I didn't care if he was fat or thin or big or small. I just wanted him *there*.

Again, it's not about how long you last or how bendy you are or about your body parts. It's about being present and loving and listening to yourself and each other.

Oh, one last thing and please don't take this the wrong way. I love men, but what's with all the poking. There's not a woman on the planet that likes to be poked. Now I'm not talking about a loving pat on the face or behind. I'm talking about when we're on the phone or doing the dishes or bending down (usually to pick up your socks), you poke us. Under the arms, up the butt, or you grab our breasts.

What are you thinking? Do you think we *like* this? This issue comes up in session all the time. Should we do this to you when you're on an important business call and about to land the Cheese Whiz account? Is this some "guy thing," like whacking the towel in the locker room? Is this some leftover from Cro-Magnon times? If you really want to love us up, there's always the Cayman Islands. I heard the weather's nice this time of year.

Optional Assignment

Look to see what you bring to all your relationships, sexual or not. If you want more love in your life, be more loving. Want sweet? Be sweet. Want compassion? Humor? Understanding? You get it. Just be what you want. The worst that could happen is, you'll be a better you.

BIRTH CONTROL

Test Your Birth Control Knowledge

True or False?

1. The VAGINAL RING is the fourth Book of the J. R. Tolkien series.

2. The PATCH is something that Captain Hook used to quit smoking.

3. A DIAPHRAGM is pictures of relief maps used in school.

4. Having your TUBES TIED is when you hook your DVD to your entertainment center.

5. A CERVICAL CAP is something the dentist uses to replace a bad molar.

6. The SPONGE removes baked-on messes like lasagna and veal scaloppini.

7. The RHYTHM METHOD is Ringo's step-by-step "how to" book on drumming.

8. The male and female CONDOM is a co-ed place one owns that's part of an association.

9. The I.U.D. is a missile that Iran is developing.

10. VASECTOMY is a Portuguese explorer who was the first to sail directly from Europe to India.

OUT OF THE BOX

This is a true story. A woman comes into my office and one of the first things she says to me after the opening "Hello" ceremonies (like the Olympics) is "I Am the Ugliest Woman that Ever Walked the Face of the Earth." I'm thinking, "Wow, that's quite a statement."

First of all, this woman was really pretty. Not in a Michelle Pfeiffer-Cameron Diaz kind of way, but in an interesting Gauguin-lush, fruity kind of way. Also she could not be "the ugliest woman who ever walked the face of the earth," because obviously she'd never been to Coney Island and seen the same Bearded Lady that came out of the Fun House that I still dream about. (It scared me so deeply that it threw off all hopes of menstruation till I was 35.)

But this woman was deadly serious.

I'm thinking to myself, "What kind of self-definition is that to walk around with? What kind of energy is that to put out there?" My belief is that we not only teach people how to treat us (we're like little mirrors reflecting back each other's thoughts), but that our beliefs and thoughts also shape the exact experiences we have in life.

So I start telling her some of my observations about thoughts and beliefs and energy and I'm going on and on, but I can see that this woman isn't buying any of it. She is convinced of her ugliness and no one was "reflecting" back anything. I tried everything to loosen her grip.

There's a thing in therapy called a "secondary gain," a "good" reason to have a problem or to think in a certain way. We looked spiritually, emotionally, energetically. We looked at old programming, decisions, and fears of being great. I told jokes, used metaphors and quotes. Nope. Nada, nothing. I was working way too hard. I clearly had to look at my own stuff and *my* need for her to change, but I even used that in the session! Finally, not without an inner struggle, I had to let her be (I'm a little slow).

Surprisingly, she called me a few days later. What happened was that the next day she was in her car at the market and some guy "with intention" drove diagonally across the parking lot, parked right next to her and motioned to her to roll down her window, which she did. He got in her face and looked her squarely in the eye and said, "YOU ARE THE UGLIEST WOMAN THAT EVER WALKED THE FACE OF THE EARTH!" I swear! Verbatim, her exact words! At first she was mortified. She could barely believe this was happening. Then she moved into total agreement. "See, I knew it!" But then it was way too absurd. What are the odds? About one in 12 bazillion? She saw. She saw how powerful she was and if she could create this, she could create anything.

Now you don't have to know anything about gravity to feel it, or see electricity to use it. The same goes for the power of thought. We may not be aware of what's in our minds, but we are still effected by its presence and power. We are like wonderful senders and receivers of the thoughts that we all carry.

This is not to say that you can't have a negative thought or the Boogeyman will get you, or that you will pull in all kinds of bad stuff. Think of it like a meditation. It's the attachment to it or the unconsciousness about it that determines what and who is running the show. I don't know about you, but just the idea of "must not have bad thoughts" makes me nervous. It's like saying, "Susan, don't eat pie." The mind just hooks on the word pie. "Pie, pie, *must* have pie." Now I'm driven. By the way, that's also one of the reasons why diets don't work. When you can't have something, you fix on it. Of course, you'll probably end up eating everything that isn't nailed down or marked "poison" in order to avoid the 200-calorie pie, and then after you've eaten the 1800 calories of not pie, you will probably eat the pie anyway and that makes 2000. The stress of it all is much worse than the pie or the thought could ever be.

There is an amazing energy, a common humanity, which links us all. This explains the invisible connections we have with one another. We've all seen and experienced it: the bonds between parents and children; between twins; with our pets, and our partners. We all possess energies that respond with one another's beliefs and thoughts.

When people come to me and want to create love in their lives, I have them write lists of exactly what they want. We clear doubts, creating certainty, and link it with emotion and vision. It's very cool. This one woman who I was working with made her list. One of the items was, "He must live in Ireland and be visiting here and then take me back with him." My first thought was, "Is this even possible?" But I was thinking *inside* the box, so I then thought, "Why not?" She could see it. She could taste it.

Shortly after, this woman met a guy (named Sean, of course, from you know where) and guess what? They fell in love and she is actually living with this man in Ireland. This one really blew my mind! It opens up a larger question. What are the limits of the human mind? What would happen if we were to think outside the box and truly believe that all is possible? Not just in our own lives, but as a planet?

Oh, and by the way, if you're thinking about what to name your children or a new business, consider the notion that not only is there energy in names, but that they have certain collective implications.

Personally, I would skip names like Saddam or Adolph or Little Mao and go more with Angel or Jesus or Krishna (Harry Krishna). Choose your names wisely. If your last name is Swine or Fink, I'd skip the name Ima.

Optional Assignment

Look at one situation in your life that you may be struggling with. It could be poor health, not enough love, not enough money. Look at the way you think and feel about it. Feeling stuck? Hopeless? Boxed in? Maybe even victimized?

Try this: pretend it's one year later and the problem was solved. That's it. You're healthy now, or wealthy, or have wonderful love. Now let yourself really feel what that's like. Play with it. How would a healthy person hold their body? What would they eat for lunch? How would someone who had plenty of love or money walk around? Would they strut? Be more playful? Stand taller? Have fun with this. Guess what? You just stepped out of the box.

"ASK YOUR DOCTOR..."

Here's the deal. "Pete" takes Propecia for male-pattern baldness. Propecia causes him dizziness, breast tenderness and enlargement, breathing difficulties, and decreased sexual ability and desire. So his hair looks fabulous but his nipples hurt, he can't breathe, and now he can't--How shall I say this?--get it up.

To remedy that, he takes Viagra. This makes him even dizzier, sensitive to light, and overwhelmingly nauseous. But the good news is that the blood flow to his penis is better than ever. So what if his vision is blurred, he's light-headed, has diarrhea, and desperately needs to lie down?

All this makes him very anxious. So "Pete" (fictional and clearly exaggerated, of course) takes Xanex. Now he's as stiff as a board, but the rest of him is way too drugged and relaxed--to the point that he's so unsteady and clumsy that he has trouble walking to the bathroom without his penis knocking over the DVD player, a couple of speakers, and the digital clock.

Sometimes, instead of Xanex, he may opt for Ambien, which causes him temporary memory loss. Which, if you think about it, might not be such a bad thing, because at least for a while he can forget that he has big lactating breasts, diarrhea, can't breathe or urinate, and that he's just wrecked over twenty-five-hundred dollars' worth of electronic equipment.

All this renders him stressed and depressed, and that's why he takes Prozac, which makes him lose his hair . . . Aaaaaah! What's going on here? Is listening and honoring our bodies totally out of the question here?

Are all medicines bad? Of course not. I'm not talking about medications that keep us healthy or balanced and thriving on the planet. I'm talking about our inability to handle discomfort. I'm talking about our need to keep doing what we're doing--our need to produce and perform, no matter what the repercussions, or what our bodies are telling us. Plus, the system that fosters and supports all this craziness is even more looney tunes.

I was talking on the phone with an insurance company, trying to convince them to cover psychotherapy for one of my clients. I couldn't believe my ears. The woman I spoke with actually said that they would only cover this guy, "If he takes medication. It's more cost effective."

Bottom line: drug companies, like insurance companies, are in business to make a profit. It's all about sales and increasing growth, and that means more volume. Either more people take drugs, or those who already do must increase their usage.

Have you watched TV lately? It's nothing short of criminal. There you are, innocently sitting in your underwear, eating frozen pizza rolls or something, watching the "Law and Order" channel and--BAM!--within one commercial break, you see the Zoloft cartoon man, the Herpes Girl, the Grandma who, thanks to some pill, can now pick up her grandchildren without peeing in her pants, the little birth control-ring lady (who looks like Mary Tyler Moore in her "Dick Van Dyke" days), and, of course, the mother who talks frankly to her daughter about douching.

Come on! We can do better than that. We are better than that. So no matter what's going on in your body, listen to it. What is it saying? Is it telling you to slow down? Take care? Eat better? Exercise? Get more light?

Communicate with yourself. Communicate with life. Appreciate it. Bless it. If you do, you won't have to call me in the morning.

Optional Assignment

If you are taking medications:

What medications are you taking out of necessity or out of habit? What medications are you taking hoping for a quick fix?

Are these meds a cover for something deeper? Don't be afraid to explore this possibility with your doctor or a health care professional.

Is your body trying to tell you something? Maybe it's time to listen.

Please note..."Pete" and side effects are obviously made up. So don't be taking, mixing or altering any medication without first consulting your doctor or heath care practitioner.

"...BY ITS COVER"

I have this stuffed cat in my office. No, not the taxidermy kind which totally creeps me out, but a very sweet, soft, stuffed animal that looks and feels incredibly real. It's amazing what I can learn by watching people handle this thing.

I once had this pierced, studded, black-leathered, chain-carrying, tough looking biker guy in my office. I think he was ordered to come by the courts. When he spoke, it was "f'ing" this and "f'ing" that. "F'ing courts," "f'ing judge," "f'ing Thursday," (yes, Thursday!). To tell you the truth, at first sight, I was *f'ing* scared of him. Anyhow, this guy sits down and starts ranting and raving about having to be here, and while he's talking, he picks up this cat, sticks it on his lap and starts stroking it in the most tender loving way. I'm thinking underneath all this House of Leather is a guy who's a sweetheart. I look at him stroking the cat; he looks at me. He is so busted, and to his credit he starts laughing.

Another time this guy comes in who is about 19 years old and struggling with issues around his sexuality. "Am I gay? Am I not gay? Is it sick? Is it not sick?" While he's talking about his conflict and how hot Tom Cruise is, he picks up the cat and starts stroking its tail. Up and down, faster and faster. How can I put this delicately? I almost had stuffing all over my office as he was bringing this thing to stuffed-animal orgasm. So he finally looks down and sees what he's doing and looks up at me and says, "I'm gay."

I've had people come in, usually after a yoga class or church or something, wearing all white or hip Indian clothes, or Jehovah Witness-looking suits. They're talking peace and love, quoting either Revelations or the Bhaga-vad-Gita, sitting there, cat on lap, strangling the crap out of the thing!

My point is this: things and people are not always what they seem. Sometimes people pretend to be some-one or someplace they are not. It's nothing that a big dose of self-love and acceptance couldn't fix. But some-times, more often than not, it is our pictures and judg-ments and need to slap labels on each other that prevent us from looking past the surface and recognizing the true reality of one another.

Here's a recent example: I'm at my neighborhood gym, there's a bunch of us there doing our thing, the TV's on--CNN, ESPN, E (or "the Brittany, Brad and Clooney Channel"). The music is playing, and Jessica Simpson is singing "Come on boots, start walking" and in spite of all this, we're all into our own little grooves. Suddenly this woman bolts in, takes all the fans and puts them on the highest it'll go (the Katrina setting). Forget toupees and tiny animals, even capped teeth are not safe at this ve-locity. She then starts to work out. We're all looking at each other judging the stuffing out of her, muttering words under our breaths like you used to hear in the old Popeye cartoons. There we are, feeling smirky and bonded in our collective disdain.

The next day at my office, I go into the waiting room and guess who my new client is? Yep, Katrina herself! I'm looking at my imaginary studio audience, which I keep in my head for situations just like this. I can't believe how beautifully life works! She walks in, sits down and starts talking. She's lovely! She's warm (apparently very), her lights are on, and she laughs at my jokes—which makes her *truly* lovely.

What is her issue? This woman is very ill. She has a disease that raises her body temperature so dramatically and to such levels of discomfort that, she says, "I start acting like a crazy person. I feel so badly for the way I'm behaving but I feel so insane."

In essence, she was asking me to help her be a better person. Me, the one who judged the bleep out of her the previous day! I guess we teach what we need to learn.

It goes both ways. Don't you hate when someone pegs you for being something or in some place you are not? How about something you used to be but are no longer? I used to have quite a little eating disorder. Let's put it this way, when I was younger I was the only kid I knew that had an open tab going with the Good Humor man. As I got older, I swung the other way. In fact, I was so anorexic that I considered lifting a toothpick an aerobic exercise. But that was about 450 years ago. To this day, some people still look at me with concern when I eat, or even if I don't eat.

Maybe you used to be chronically late, or drink like a fish, or your ethics were *way* out there. Let's give each other a little credit for our growth. Let's slow down and be more open and compassionate. Let's do less judging and be gentler with one another.

So the next time someone cuts you off on the freeway, before you blow your horn or your top or your cool, consider this: that person may be late to their little Timmy's debut as a snowflake in the Christmas school pageant.

Optional Assignment

Have you made assumptions in the past? Have some of them been incorrect? Do you come to the people in your life with fresh eyes each day? Do you truly know who they are? Do you truly know who you are?

See if you can suspend your judgments for one whole day. Really, try it. Once you do, your heart will open to boundless possibilities, and that's where all the fun begins.

ON HELPING

I like to think I'm a problem solver, but when Annie came to see me 20-plus years ago, I didn't know what to do.

Annie, then in her early 20's, was stunning. She had the kind of beauty that would throw Catherine Zeta-Jones into therapy. I adored her immediately. She was smart, articulate, funny, sweet, and adventurous. As if that wasn't enough, she was an accomplished ballet dancer.

Annie was also going blind. She was a child diabetic and had already lost her sight in one eye. After numerous surgeries, the little pinhole of sight left in the other eye was rapidly diminishing.

I did no "therapy" with Annie. Someone would drive her to my office three times a week and she would just cry and I would just hold her. It broke my heart. I was so saddened, angry, and frustrated for her. I felt impotent and completely useless.

As the weeks went on, I noticed that my own body started feeling terrible. My chest ached and so did my arms and my shoulders. I was literally holding her grief and taking on her pain. I'm surprised I didn't go blind in the process.

Up until that point, I didn't understand what helping or supporting someone really meant. When I saw pain, I wanted to fix it. I saw that when I joined someone, there was great relief, and they didn't feel so alone. But what I didn't know was that there was a big difference between *holding* the space for someone's pain versus *sharing* in it or taking it on.

So there I was, trying to make it better, but going down like a B-17 in a bad WW II movie. Then one day I had an epiphany that enabled me to release all the drama around the event. I thought, "Maybe there's a rightness to this. Maybe this is perfect. Maybe she's supposed to be the best blind dancer the world has ever known." Or, "Maybe she's supposed to help other child diabetics through this process." Or, "Maybe this is karmic." How do I know? But something felt very right about it. So right, in fact, that my body immediately felt better, as if I had an instant healing on some evangelist channel.

From then on, things felt different. I was able to be with Annie in a whole new way. In time, I told her what had happened, and it wasn't long before Annie began shifting too. The irony was that by removing myself from the drama of it, I became more loving, more present. I didn't have to fix her. I just had to be with her. There was her life, and then there was her situation. In other words, there was Annie, and then there was the stuff she was going through. Holding things in this context not only changed how I was in the room, but also completely changed how I am in the world.

I had another client-"teacher" around the same time. Joe used to come into my office week after week telling me how bad his marriage was, how his wife was this and that, how they were constantly fighting, etc. So each week Joe comes in all stressed out and each week he walks out feeling a little bit better.

Then I went on vacation. Two weeks later, Joe walks into my office and he looks absolutely vibrant. He's relaxed and alive. I said, "Wow! You look amazing. What happened?" He says, "Well, you weren't here to talk to and take the edge off so I was left alone with her. Just me and her. After a week, I couldn't stand it anymore. I knew there was no repairing this. I just knew I had to leave. So I did. It feels right, and I feel pretty darn good."

"Wow," I thought again. My "helping" was keeping this guy stuck. My "helping" was keeping him from experiencing the full impact of his life. My "helping" is so *not* helping.

Am I saying, "Don't help"? Heck no. On the contrary, look around. This place could use all the love and help we can muster. What I am saying is, look at how and why we help.

I tried to "help" a spider out of my bathroom the other day. In the process I broke at least six of his legs in at least twelve different places trying to get him into a coleslaw container so I could get him safely outside. Sometimes helping is about just opening a door and completely getting out of the way.

Oh, and by the way, Annie didn't go blind. She went back to school and got degrees in business and psychology. She now runs an extraordinary center for children who are diabetic. She is a powerful, graceful, and incredibly gifted woman, and, boy, can she dance.

Optional Assignment

Look to see if your "helping" is actually really helping. For example, if you are supporting an able adult child who is old enough not only to remember Eisenhower but also knew him personally, you might want to rethink it and let "Junior" fend for himself.

Your experience may or may not be this overt but nonetheless, stop a moment and look behind how and why you are helping.

Allow yourself to pop out of your situation and write the script. What happens if I continue helping in this way? What might happen if I stopped? In the long run, does your helping really serve the greater good?

FASTER!

Just got back from Comedy Traffic School and all I can say is, "Oy vey." Even the Chinese girl and the guy from Kenya sitting next to me said, "Oy vey."

First of all, you'd think Comedy Traffic School would at least be better than the regular kind. At least with the regular kind you don't come with expectations of smiling and having a good time. No offense to this older gentleman who ran the class, but if I were to have a choice between a series of rabies shots or eight hours of "Comedy" Traffic School, no question I'd pick the shots. There was not even an attempt to be funny, like before the drunk driving film which begged for some kind of line like, "take my life, please," or "my tires are so fat (or flat) . . ." No! Nada! Nothing!

I should have known right away when I first looked at the blackboard and the instructor's name was Robert White, not even "Bob," and forget Chuckles or Shecky. I felt like I was back in elementary school. You know, when you look up at that big school clock and its only 9:43 a.m., then you get interested in a fly or something and think, "Well, that was at least 20-minutes worth" only to find that it's just 9:44.

OK, so after counting all the teeth in my head with my tongue and all the brunettes in the room, I cleaned out my purse, gave everyone around me mints and toothpicks (they were so grateful I could have sold them for five bucks a piece), it was finally 10:03. By the way, did you know that if you sit in a folding chair long enough, half your butt can fall asleep while the other half is still awake? So there you are, stuck in a class that's so cold I'm sure the average sperm count of all the men in the room was lowered by 50%. You're captive. The only thing different from this class and my version of Hell is that you don't need gloves and a muffler in Hell.

Why am I telling you this, and why was I there? I was speeding and, truthfully, I'm surprised it took me this long to get caught. Why was I speeding? Well, like most of us, I'm rushing around like a lunatic trying to do too many things, barely leaving enough time for anything out of the ordinary to happen - like life. By the way, you ever notice how on the freeway traffic stops only to find that people were checking out a towel or a paper bag on the side of the road? Why? What are they thinking? Or worse yet, when there's really been an accident and your first re- sponse is, "Good, now I can get going"!?!

Besides the speeding, I multi-task. I use my cell phone, make appointments, put on lipstick--(gotta watch out for those pot holes; I once looked like a hooker on Quaaludes)--I sing, play harmonica (great to Dylan and early Beatles, especially "Love Me Do"), and if that's not bad enough, I weave in and out like a drunk Indy racer. In essence, I'm an accident waiting to happen.

This is so not good. So for me, this class was a gift. A chance to change. Plus it was like aversion therapy. Be- tween the fee for the class, $31 bucks, and the ticket, $182 bucks, and the eight hours with Mr. Potato Head, I'm a changed person now, driving in the middle lane listening to music that only dentists and gynecologists play.

So I got to thinking about our way of living and how

everything is getting faster and faster. Fast cars, fast news, fast relief. Yes, I know sometimes fast is good, like when it comes to getting a root canal, or fun, like jet-skiing or roller coasters, but what's the rush? What's the hurry? I'm all for high speed this and high-tech that, but all this rushing around is insane and the price we pay is ridiculous, not to mention alienating and dangerous. It's not only compromising our health, but our relationship to ourselves and to each other.

I can see instant oatmeal, instant coffee, even instant karma, but instant childhood? Instant story books? What, "Green Eggs, No Ham"? Fast food has its place, but preparing and eating food used to be an art form - a way of life. If Da Vinci was alive today he'd paint "The Fast Supper," instead of "The Last Supper."

And if that's not bad enough, now there's no rest. You can learn while you sleep. Yes, you can wake up exhausted from lack of R.E.M. and be cranky in 12 different languages.

I think it's time to slow down. When we rush we tend to only experience what's on the surface, but by giving ourselves the gift of time it allows us to taste life in all its fullness.

I might add that slowing down has some mighty fine benefits too. We are free to enjoy the moment, make meaningful and mindful connections--spiritually, emotionally and physically--to each other, to nature, to art, and to our hearts. Not bad.

Oh, by the way, here are some other things you don't want to be doing while driving: Don't spay or neuter anything or, for that matter, attempt any kind of surgical procedure. Don't shave, especially your legs, make banana daiquiris, iron, paint, watch "E.R.," or take a home pregnancy test.

Optional Assignment

For one day, get rid of the clock. Eat when you're hungry. Sleep if you're tired. Walk, talk—kiss, if desired. Allow yourself to listen to your natural rhythms. Much better, don't you think?

ON SILENCE

I had a sobering experience about seven or eight years ago. Not the Betty Ford, detox, A.A. sobering kind, but the life changing you-gotta-be-kidding, "Help Me Rhonda," "Oy Vey: the Book, the Movie and the Musical"-sobering kind. Here's what happened...

You know how people have that sexy whispering voice? Well, I woke up one day and sounded like that - sore throaty, sex-hotline sounding. I'm thinking, "OK, I guess this is what laryngitis is," and of course I immediately wanted to change my answering machine. "Hi...this is Susan...Ooooh...you know what to do..." But as the day went on, I intuitively felt something was definitely wrong. By the end of the day, my voice went from sounding like Lauren Bacall in "The Big Sleep" to Darth Vader, double reedy and very breathy.

Personally, I'm natural in my approach to life and not a big fan of doctors, but given my foreboding sixth sense, I went straight to the Vatican: the ear, nose and throat specialist in Beverly Hills, California. It's amazing what you'll do when fear runs the show. I just hope when it comes down to it that I'm not the person pushing old people and babies out of the way to get to the lifeboat.

Anyhow, this guy checks my throat every which way. He puts everything down there: cameras--he went in there, the nurse went in there, the entire fourth floor...--

29

everything. Then he looks up at me and says, "Your vocal chord is paralyzed. " I said, "_ _ _ _ !" (By that time, nothing was coming out.) Then he said, "98-percent of people who have this kind of paralysis never get their voice back." You know those moments in life where you get all hot and your crotch goes down to your feet? This was definitely one of them. "Oh God," I thought. "_ _ _ _ _!" I said. Then something clicked inside of me. My whole being went, "No Way!" But it came out " _ _ _ _ _ !" I thought, "How dare you put that out to me! Watch me, you ____ hole or head (you fill in the blank)."

I will skip ahead because now I can speak and shout and sing (my dancing, not so good), but it took almost six months to just get a sound out and almost a year to sing (I make a great Tony from "West Side Story"). Boy, it was truly sobering.

This is not a "poor me" story. Believe me, compared to most, I am a lucky pig. This was my first introduction to silence, which, coming from a New York Jewish background is more foreign than eating pork, hunting and buying retail combined.

It was stressful and frustrating at first to say the least, especially when I was outside. I felt vulnerable with no voice. Could I get help if I needed it? Asking directions was completely out of the question (Hey, I'm a girl.) So was a simple, "Hi" or "Good morning" (so I perfected the guy nod, you know, slight jerk with the head and no eye contact). When I tried to speak, the little that did come out sounded hideous. People thought I was retarded. They'd say, "H - E - L - L - O. . .H - O - W. . .A – R - E. . .Y - O - U. . .?" And loud, like if they could hear it in the Philippines somehow I would too. AHH! I felt crazy, so isolated and totally misunderstood! My heart cried with compassion for people that are handicapped in this society and raged at the stupidity of the rest of us. But as frustrated as I was, silence was becoming my teacher.

I began seeing that most of what came out of my mouth was about my discomfort with silence. It felt too naked. My incessant talking was a way to fill the void. I saw how my personality and jokes were most often coming from a place to get people either to like me or regard me in a certain way. I saw that talking was a way to control, to feel safe. I saw that words can actually push us apart, connecting us only from a small portion of our heads, instead of full out with our hearts. I couldn't sing. I couldn't speak. Even the voice in my head began to quiet. It was such a. . .*RELIEF*!

Noise has taken over our lives. Instead of listening to our inner soul, to nature and each other, we are listening to a drone of 24-hour perky, news casting, talk-showy experts pushing fast relief, cubic zirconium and long lasting Viagra (you really want to watch that last one, especially if you travel coach).

All this noise is beside the point and leaves us emptier and emptier. If you are having trouble in your life, stop talking. If you are having problems in your relationships, stop talking. In silence there is so much depth and sweetness to be had. In stillness there is everything.

Optional Assignment

Take one day out of your life and get silent. Surrender to it. Let it surround and enter you. At first your mind will seem as noisy as a Chihuahua on amphetamines, but hang in there. Just allow it.

In time the volume decreases, and you'll find that you've become more present and more peaceful. The

31

bottom line: it's what's inside of our own heads that makes the world so truly noisy.

"EVERYTHING'S UNDER CONTROL"

I just had this little kid in my office. I will call him Da-mien—(not his real name, which is probably Lucifer). Now I'm all for fostering wonder and curiosity and discovery in both adults and children, but this kid had his hands on everything and I swear, in less than a nano-second my entire office was trashed by this Chucky on steroids.

Let's put it this way. I now know what A.D.D. stands for: Agent for Demo and Destruction. Of course it's not OK for anyone to trash or disrespect any person or place, but what demon-boy did show me, and I'm not proud of this, is how much this one little encounter could really wig me out.

Truth is, I know I'm a control freak in certain ways, es-pecially when it comes to my environment. But I pretend I'm not. So if you came to my house, I wouldn't vacuum while you're still there, but if you were in the restroom for a while... No really, I'm working on it. I do know that straight-ening the bed during lovemaking may not be the place I want to come from. Anyway, I really thought I had let a lot of my anal-ocity go and I had gotten pretty relaxed about things until devil-boy showed up.

I see now that disguised underneath my use of words like "harmony," "minimalism," "zen," etc., was still a raging lunatic. Let's say in the middle of the night the wind blew my Feng Shui-ed paper lantern on its side. As pathetic as it sounds, I'd feel compelled to get out of bed and fix it. Of course I'd pretend I was on my way to the bathroom as I gently kicked it into place. OK, so little Freddy Krueger got me thinking. What is control? And the mother of all questions: Is there really such a thing anyway?

Probably the need to control comes from our sense of helplessness or powerlessness. Especially in our culture, it feels way too vulnerable to let go, to not know and still trust. The kicker is that sometimes letting go of control not only doesn't result in powerlessness but also opens us up to a deeper experience of trust and connection, and the power in that is both thrilling and spectacular.

What can we really control anyway? The whole setup is such that everything is impermanent and ultimately uncontrollable.

Let's face it, jobs come and go, spouses come and go (and in some cases, come and go and come and go and...). Also, we age no matter what we do. At my age (that's 54 with makeup) all my peers are spreading. I can do sit-ups 24/7 and at some point no matter how many I do, I will still end up looking like my Russian ancestors, furry and round, like fruit. I went for a run not too long ago and I kept hearing this sound. I couldn't figure out what it was. My shoes? My hat? No, it was my arms flapping in the wind. That's right. O.K., so I started to work out a little at the gym. Now my muscular arms flap in the wind. Forget about it. I can't control anything. And gravity, I don't think so. I looked down at the skin on my legs the other day. Not only did I have hundreds of new spots that I didn't have three days earlier, but it also looked like an inverted night sky (I'm my own planetarium). I swear it looked like I was wearing pants.

34

Most everything is out of our control. Health comes and goes, money, friends, things, and moments. The truth is, the more we try to hang on, the further it is pulled from our reach. The irony is that our attempt to control only causes more stress, pain, and suffering.

It's all about letting go. I know, easier said than done. But think about it. What's the measure of a great relationship? Being and giving your best and being willing to let go. No one's in control. It's about just being with and for each other.

Is there anything we *can* control? I guess all we've got is how we hold things: our actions, reactions, non-reactions, attitudes, words to ourselves and others, and our ethics. And for some of us, our relationship to something greater than ourselves, like keeping an open heart to the wonder in and around us all.

Have I mastered any of this yet? Obviously not, as my reaction to the Little Prince of Darkness showed. Also, I must admit, there is still a part of me that wants to control things, because if there is such a thing as heaven, mine would be very orderly: 72-degrees, made out of chocolate, and have crisp clean sheets.

Optional Assignment

Take a moment and make a list of all the things you are trying to control. Read it. Look to see how much energy it takes to keep all this going. Now, look at each item. Ask yourself two questions. How important is it? And what would happen if you let it go?

Select one thing off your list. Make it an easy one. See if you'd be willing to release it for one week. I think you might like what could happen.

35

DUTY FREE

I just got back from visiting my folks in Florida. Not the cool Florida where people vacation at fancy hotels with ice sculptures, pink flamingos, and big fountains. Or the school break, g-string-topless Florida where kids go to tan, drink beer, and grope one another. Not even the New York-New Jersey Florida where chopped liver costs more than Beluga caviar, and bagels and matzo balls are used successfully as floatation devices. No, the redneck Alabama part of Florida.

Let's put it this way, the Gun and Ammo store is right next to Liquor Barn and directly across the street from Hooters, and, of course, the *EEK-A-BOO OTEL*.

I think my parents are the only Jews within a hundred miles of this place. But what's nice is that the sweet guy at the Piggly-Wiggly Market tries his best and puts out boxes of matzo for them every time there's a Jewish holiday, even Yom Kippur.

Getting to them is a whole other story because flying has become ridiculous. Between the long lines, early check-ins and security, it now takes longer to fly from California to Florida than it does to get a real estate license or pass the bar exam. And how come all nonstop flights leave before 7 a.m.? Or if you want to sleep in past 3 a.m., you have to change planes in Phoenix, Brazil, and Texas.

So there you are, 5 a.m., showing your drivers license

83 times. What could possibly go on from the bottom of the escalator to the top? Personally, since I look like a drug-smuggling heroin addict in my I.D. picture (my boyfriend looks like the "Unabomber"), I invariably get the once over with that loud wand that even a filling could set off--and that's after pretty much disrobing before the human x-ray machine.

You ever notice they don't even look at the screen after you've taken off your shoes, belt, earrings, and the metal plate in your head? Having gone through all that trouble, you'd think they could at least take a look.

And what's with all the new rules? Come on, please, whose making all this up? They're probably all stoned, laughing their heads off. . . "OK, let's see, they can take a vibrator and some Mentos, but no herring or pickup sticks."

Here's what you can bring: three oz. or less of Neosporin, bug repellent, and over the counter canker sore cream. "Yes" on cigar cutters, corkscrews, personal lubricants, butter knives, knitting needles and gel bras (gel shoe inserts: not OK!?).

"No" on ice picks, meat cleavers, sabers, all swords, bows and arrows, pool cues (unless you can prove your name is "Fats"), brass knuckles, hand grenades (darn), cattle prods, or tools over seven inches--finally, great news for some of you guys out there.

No beverages from home, but "yes" on cheese (?), duty free alcohol, whipped-cream, and a-ok on chocolate pudding.

And they take stuff away from you. What, I'm gonna hijack the plane with my eyeglass repair tools or my new Halle Berry make-up kit? And what do they do with all the stuff they confiscate anyway? You ever notice how soft and youthful everyone's hands are becoming in customs?

So you're up for eight hours, gone to the Gift Shop 14 times where the same pack of almonds you passed up at the market the day before for $2.50 is now $18.75, and you're finally ready to board the plane...by zones. Of course you're in zone nine and they start with zone one and you're frantically looking to see the zone on the boarding pass of the baby crying next to you.

Then there's more checking of the ID's to see if you've picked up a bomb or a nuclear device since they last checked three minutes earlier.

OK, you're finally on and usually sitting next to someone who loves to talk or smells like they've been marinating in the kind of cologne they used to make for game shows in the '60s.

No. The pleasure trip doesn't stop there. No longer are there free movies and snacks and meals being offered, and unless you've just run a marathon and are dangerously low on sodium, I wouldn't be shelling out $4.50 for that pretzel-nut-cheese thing. Also, who wants to sit five hours all cranked up on the coffee and sugar products that they do supply?

What happened to a little comfort, a little kindness, not to mention our basic human rights? The movie is five bucks (do they have some kind of deal with Ben Affleck?). It's either that or the "SkyMall Magazine." I actually found myself thinking and considering the Sumo Wrestler glass top coffee table. The best is the plane sheets--personal airline seat covers - which begs the question, What the heck have I been sitting in?

OK, no food, no water, and I paid almost $400 for this? After the turbulence, the lack of sustenance, the crying baby, the woman on amphetamines and the guy with TB who just coughed on me, I'm whipped.

Here's the deal. Something is very wrong with this picture. Does it have to be this way? The nature of our diminishing freedoms happened well before 9/11. In order to make sure that terrorism doesn't strike again, certain restrictions have been put into place, perhaps keeping us safer, but at what cost?

There are Big Brother cameras on most corners in England and now throughout New York City. There is now a thing called a "terror score" designed to identify high risk travelers, tracking information like where you are from or if you pay in cash or buy a one-way ticket.

Being monitored and taking freedoms away feels really creepy to me. Plus, the more we live from a place of fear and isolation, the more we perpetuate fear and isolation.

I'm all for being conscious and vigilant, but maybe we need to shift to a higher purpose of vision and balance so our children may flourish. If not, they may inherit a dark world of arbitrary laws and regulations without benefit from the light and humanity of the human heart.

Optional Assignment

Let's look at our own lives. Is there balance in your life between prudent prevention and unbounded anxiety? If your stomach is continually in knots, that may be the tip-off to being too fear based. Are there things that you can change to hold your life more loosely? It's about being smart, aware, and being able to enjoy your moments all at the same time.

ON BEAUTY

Is it getting really freaky out there or is it just me? I recently had a lady in my office with oodles of Botox injected into her forehead and around her eyes. You know the stuff. It's called botulinum toxin, type a. It's the same toxin that causes food poisoning and interferes with the muscles ability to contract, rendering them pretty much paralyzed. By the way, you don't want to inject this stuff near your lips, unless you think looking fabulous includes drooling on your pants.

She also had tons of, I think, collagen or helium or something all around her mouth, making her look like a female incarnation of The Joker or a float in the Macy's Day Parade. So she now has this permanent frozen grin on her face. No matter what she talks about, I just see this grin. "I'm so angry." Grin. "My husband just ran off with the secretary at his law firm." Grin. I'm thinking, "Apparently, the secretary is now handling this guy's briefs." (Now *I'm* grinning.) All I can see is this blank face and this funny looking grin. My head is starting to spin and I'm having a hard time computing all this. In times like this, and for comic relief and my own sanity, I look again to the studio audience I have in my own mind.

The last straw was when a distressed 16 year old came into my office after her nose job. The night before, she had spotted two little lines on the bridge of her nose.

41

The Botox she had received was just not doing the job. I thought, "She's 16! What's next for kids, an instant McFace Lift from Ronald McDonald?"

I had another woman come in who had fat repositioning. That's when you take the fat from one part of your body--in this case, her behind--and put it someplace else, in her case, on her entire head!

When I first saw her, she looked odd with a big fat face on her skinny skinny body, like a Tootsie-Roll pop. But she was just loving the look. What could I say? So yet again, I looked to my studio audience.

What's going on here? Has the world gone wild? Half of us are starving or fleeing bombs, while the rest of us are repositioning our faces and body parts. Is it just a deflection that comes from feeling overwhelmed? Or, do we really think that lifting our butts will improve the quality of our lives?

Hey, wear your butts on your back if it makes you happy. I'm all for anyone who wants to defy gravity.

There's tummy tucks, body contouring--after the gastric-bypass surgery, of course--cellulite correction, scarless facelifts (who, besides pirates or Freddy, would go for the one *with* the scar?), leg vein treatments. There are also various "fillers" for wrinkles like Botox, Restylane and Sculptura (I think I made ashtrays out of that in camp). You can remove the bags and dark circles under your eyes, so pretty much you can still continue to do crack and drink with no tell-tale signs of liver damage.

What's with us? Can't we leave well enough alone? Is aging gracefully totally out of the question?

How about liposuction? By the way, you definitely don't want to watch that procedure on TV or the entire Surgery Channel, for that matter. Whose idea is this anyway? "Let's put Bob's testicles on TV. Let's watch as they supersize Mary from a 32-A to a 46-triple D."

Personally, I'm not above any of this craziness. My boyfriend and I now lay down flat on our backs every time we talk. We look much younger that way. And when we stroke each others' faces, we now only stroke in circular upward motions. I now see the beauty in why the older we get, the worse our eyesight becomes. But the truth is we are not our bodies and this is not who we truly are. Look inside. Does any of this really matter?

Here's an ad I recently saw in a magazine: *Bigger is Better: Safe, Proven Penile Enlargement*, as seen on the Learning Channel. That's right, the *Learning* Channel. On the opposite page, another ad read: *Vaginal Reconstruction: Repositioning and Tightening*. You figure it out.

Optional Assignment

When you look at animals, plants, or clouds, do you pick out what's wrong or do you just accept and appreciate them for what they are?

Write down what's right and beautiful and unique about what and who you are. Do include the physical. Don't just say, "I'm a nice person" or "I enjoy a nice pickle." Go for it. Allow yourself to look at your eyes and also into your eyes.

Let the appreciation unfold. Do this each day for one week. Let the healing begin with you!

GOSSIP

- *JESUS AND MARY'S SECRET LAS VEGAS WEDDING!*

- *KLUM AND SEAL GIVE BIRTH TO OTTER!*

- *BLOOD FOUND IN HUMAN BODY!*

- *CONDOLEEZA RICE AND TIM CURRY'S IN-STANT ONE MINUTE ROMANCE!*

- *SPONGE BOB'S PLOT TO RUIN HEATHER'S MARRIAGE!*

- *SCOOBIE-DOO BLAMED FOR PORN STAR'S DEATH!*

So here I am, standing in line at the market, pretending (to whom I don't know) that I'm not really reading this stuff, but really reading it. You know what I mean. This can be done easily with either a pair of dark sunglasses or using the head down - eyes up way of reading, which I perfected from years of looking at the smart girl's test paper next to me in High School.

Anyway, why am I, like so many, compelled to read this garbage? What's up with that? And besides, what's the psychology behind the entire "check-out" area? "Check out" is an understatement. On one side you got your magazines: *Star, People, Shape, Us, Self, Oui, Me, Cosmo, O, Ho*?, and your impulse items like batteries, razors, W-D 40 (Don't ask), Cheez-its, Neosporin, Xtra Strength Rolaids and assorted Beef Sticks (Never ask).

Then on the other side, you have a whole entire wall of Snickers, M&M's and 23 different kinds of Peanut Butter and Chocolate combos. And for those of us that are too lazy to bite and chew, we now have these cute little tiny pieces that can, let's face it, potentially lodge deep in your throat requiring some kind of Heimlich maneuver. And to make matters worse, when I'm not reading about O.J's Alien Baby and desperately turning to page 48 to find out the foods that actually make us *lose* weight, I'm looking in everyone's basket and making up stories about them.

Mmmmm, let's see...

...*Oreos, 9 boxes of low-carb low-sugar dietetic Fudge Bars, Advil...* (Just got her period).

...*Double-Stuffed Oreos, 14 different kinds of bread* (can't decide), *9 boxes of Rice Crispies, 11 gallons of milk...* (Stoned).

...*8 frozen family-size pizzas, 6 gallons of ice cream, diet soda, 20 rolls of toilet paper...* (Bulimic).

...*8 frozen family-size pizzas, 6 gallons of ice cream, REGULAR soda, 3 rolls of toilet paper...* (Family of 16).

I know. Sadly, I'm part of the problem.

OK, so let's talk about gossip and our obsession and curiosity about other people's lives. Well, certainly we gossip for many reasons. For one thing, it's entertaining. We also gossip in hope of shared intimacy. It can seemingly bring us together. It can lift us up as well as separate (like my bra). Some of us even take great pride in holding the secrets of others; it's a sign of both honor and trust.

There's all kinds of gossip. We gossip about people in our lives, like bosses, co-workers, neighbors, and family members. Most every family has someone they love to gossip about. You know, the Aunt with the 500 cats, or the crazy scary Uncle who keeps taking out his teeth and other removable body parts (he's usually the same guy who can turn his eyelids inside out). By the way, if you don't know who that family member is, sorry to be the one to say this, but you're probably it.

Then there's celebrity gossip, where famous people become our personal friends. To tell the truth, I get all creeped out when people start referring to them by their first name, like "Lance said...," or "Paris says...". Some of us know more about J. Lo or Jacko or Bono than the actual people in our own lives. We seem to love this stuff. Besides the tabloids, look at the popularity of our interview and talk shows, like Letterman or Leno (Dave and Jay). "What's it like sleeping with a Siberian Husky?", or "How long have you been on the South Park Diet?" Why do we care? Is it escapism so we don't have to deal with our own lives?

And what's with our obsession with dead people, like James Dean and Marilyn and Elvis? I don't get it. Are they immortalized because they tragically died at their peak? What if they had lived? In our youth obsessed culture they'd probably be tucked away in some home in Arizona or making guest appearances on "Maury" or "Celebrity Poker."

Now let's look at our daily lives. Will putting others down really raise our own feelings of respect and self worth? Will talking negatively about someone ultimately make us feel better, instead of directly talking to the person that we have issues with? As tempting as all this is, does it really make us feel good about ourselves when we do this?

You get my point. Like any obsession or addiction, it's all a deflection. I'd much rather focus on the Da Vinci Code Diet (I actually really saw this) or Goofy's Viagra nightmare than look at what's really going on in my own life. The truth is that the more we look within and take responsibility for our own feelings and actions, the less need we'll have to focus on what's trivial and the sweeter this place will be.

Oh, and by the way, don't tell my boyfriend, but I think I'm carrying a magnetic alien baby. How do I know this? Well, first of all my middle is sticking way out (though it could be the nightly 4 a.m. Meat Lover's Pizzas) and secondly, besides the fork, stapler and toaster clinging to my stomach, no matter what, I keep pointing north.

Optional Assignment

For one week, try talking up people. Tell everyone all the good stuff about the people in your lives. Talk about what's right about them and what they mean to you. Applaud their accomplishments and take joy in their successes. Go ahead, throw yourself into the mix. Everything we say has an energy to it.

ONE MOMENT PLEASE . . .

"**P**lease listen closely because our menu has changed. If you want cable TV, press #1, the Internet, press #2, Billing, press #3"--(you know you'll be holding for a month and a half on that one)—"breaking up with your boyfriend, press #4, with your girlfriend, #5, changing locations, #6, changing socks, #7…or, you could go back to the main menu"--(which, for me, always conjures up pictures of food).

By the way, if they ask if you would like to find out about their "new products" or "add a service," go for it, you'll get someone on the line in no time.

The worst is when you have to speak your selection to a machine, like "operator, please." "Sorry, we did not get that." "OPERATOR!" "Sorry, we…" (Meanwhile, they heard you in *Italy*.) Then within seconds, you are reduced to a crazy person and you start yelling, "OPERATOR! OPERATOR! OPERATOR!"

OK, you finally get through, hoping your neighbors didn't hear you. The phone starts ringing and you get all excited and start rehearsing in your mind what you need to say, like "How come I only get Nick at Night and T.V.Land and my bill says, $1,206 for the month of February?" So it rings and rings and then finally… *click*, you get another machine. "We're experiencing a high volume of calls right now"--(it's 4 in the morning)--"you could either go to *www.monopoly.we've got you over a barrel or don't bend over.com*, or you can call back another time."

So you weigh your choices. Internet's out, you need a real live person. Plus, you've already invested six minutes into this call, so you think it's just a matter of time. Then comes the music. I don't know about you, but 18 minutes of Flight of the Bumblebee does something nasty to me and I start feeling like I just snorted adrenaline or took too much growth hormone or bad diet pills. And it doesn't stop there. It goes on and on and on until you start bargaining with yourself like, "five more minutes and I'm gonna hang up," but you're hooked because it's already been 27 minutes and it could be any second now. Besides, you're so hyped up and pissed off, that now it's the principle of the thing.

OK, finally!! After the "your call may be monitored" speech, you actually get someone! You know you've got a choice here. Do you unload over 30 minutes of built up rage on this poor person or do you politely tell them what you've been through and how much ice cream you've just eaten? But before you can get anything out, not even the last four of your social or your mother's maiden name, you notice the connection is just awful. Then you realize you've been out-sourced and routed to India and the voice says, "Hello, this is Ranjit Gupta," and you can't understand a word their saying.

Now I don't want to be rude or politically incorrect but I could have sworn he said, "I'll pray for you," which I'm thinking is real nice, but it turned out he was asking about "pay per view." It kept getting crazier and crazier. All I wanted was the movie channel. A little Discovery or Animal Planet would also be nice. But then, it got beyond surreal and I had no idea what I was signing up for. I just "prayed" I didn't end up with Lifetime (the feminine hygiene channel), the Military or the Playboy Channel En Espanol. After a while, I finally started getting the hang of it and figured out that "Brahma" meant Drama and that the "Om" Box Office was really just HBO.

Just when I was about to seal the deal...I was disconnected.

Now, this is not about my little cable company. This is about what we've become. So what happened to us and how did we get here? Through our evolution towards globalization (some might call it devolution), businesses are streamlined down to the point where it's no longer financially viable or expedient to talk to a live human being. Though what globalization does promise to do, is to tie the world together--which is great. But I'm wondering, Does it have to be so depersonalizing? Is there still a way to keep it human and really help one another? At least put personalities into the machines. "If you'd like mothering, press #1, positive affirmations #2, motivation #3, empathy #4..."

People come into my office feeling isolated, angry, and helpless. I completely understand. All I can offer up to you is this: look to yourself. See how you can make your life simpler, more humane, and less dependent on technology. Believe it or not, we are all part of the solution.

Optional Assignment

For one day this week, drop out. No e-mails, computer, telephone, TV--no nothing. Can you read a book? Can you write? Play an instrument? Ride a bike? Hang with family or friends? It's about reconnecting to yourself, nature, each other, and to the miracle of life. "Bravo!" (and I don't mean the cable channel).

51

PART II.
GETTING TO KNOW YOU

ON DATING OR FINDING THE RIGHT MATE

Factoids – U.S. Bureau of Census (2004)

- *Number of unmarried and single Americans 15 and over - 95.7 million.*

- *Never been married - 63%*

- *Divorced - 23%*

- *Widowed - 14%*

There are maybe 12 trillion books written on this subject (conservative estimate). There's Mars and Venus dating, gay dating, not-so-gay dating, and in the South, there's cousin dating. There are books on "Women Who Love Too Much," "Not Enough," "Balding Accountants and the Women Who Love Them," "The Do's and Don'ts of Dating" (*don't* take heroin on the first date; *do* stick with the chilled red wine).

A lot of these books set the tone and support the myths about how we should be, look, and act on dates. Guys should pay up the nose for a very expensive meal at Chez Ritz Crackiér, where women of course eat only one leaf of lettuce (only to go home later that night and raid and pillage the fridge in such a frenzy that even

Fido's not safe). Guys, of course, would be perfectly happy to eat the same meal they had for breakfast--cold pizza and a moonpie.

All that aside, there really is a very simple way to be yourself and attract exactly what you are looking for. It starts with "The List." The way to manifest exactly what you want is to get clear on exactly what you want. Look at the experience you want to have with your partner. What is really important to you? Do you want sweet, kind, funny? The father/mother of your children? Do you even want children? Do you care about money, health, activity level, spirituality? Look at the life stage you're in. Do you want to travel? Settle down?

Allow yourself to really look at life and the partner you want. Look at ethics, sexuality, intellect. Get really specific, even if they must be a great limbo dancer. This is the most important part: get really clear *before* you get emotionally attached. When you go out there, look at a person's actions. Do they do what they say? Pay their bills? Call people back? How are their other relationships?

Don't forget to look at yourself. Are you great partner material? When was the last time you took a risk, or bettered yourself, or told the truth, or kept your word-- especially to yourself? You get the point.

Now, look at how you walk around. What is your energy saying? Are you available, loveable, approachable? If kids and dogs are scared of you, chances are this may not work in your favor.

You can meet people anywhere. From Trader Joe's to Rodeos. Where would your beloved be? If you want a Mormon experience, I think strip clubs and lap dancing are out. Some people feel comfortable placing ads. You gotta be careful about that and *definitely* learn the lingo. For instance, what does LBJ mean? Latin Bi-Sexual Jesuit? Large Black Jew? Be careful. You could be getting a fifty year old who supported the Vietnam War. I also wouldn't be placing a personal ad and selling a house at the same time. Although a three-car garage may be a nice feature, it may be misconstrued.

The opportunities are infinite. There's the Internet. You can take a class. Join a club or a gym. Ladies, if you're looking for a man, you'd do much better at Rocky's Gym or The House of Sweat than the Pilates class at Total Woman.

Here's the real truth about dating. Dating is like ice cream. If you like Mint Chip and you're dating Chocolate Swirl, it's just not your flavor. No hard feelings. Don't try to change Chocolate Swirl into Mint Chip. It ain't gonna happen. Conversely, if someone is looking for Tutti-Fruitty and you're a Coconut Surprise, it's not personal. Coconut Surprise is great, you're just not Tutti-Fruitty (Go Rooty).

So go out there. Be your wonderful self. Get clear. Stay conscious. But watch out for Chubby Hubby and definitely Rocky Road.

Optional Assignment

Get busy and write your list. By the way, if you want to manifest anything in your life, this is exactly how you do it. Get clear, be deliberate. Just know, there's plenty of love out there for you. You deserve it!

WHAT'S YOUR SIGN?

Dear Dr. Pomeranz,
    I am a Vegan Libra who just found Jesus. I am into organic gardening, macramé, folk singing and making the planet a better place. I just met a triple Scorpio who lives on McMeat, won't tell me the "firm" he works for (his x-tension is 666), loves hunting, Heavy Metal, and thinks "Holy Week" has something to do with the playoffs. Do we have a chance?
    peace,
    Rainbow Beansprout

Dear Sprout,
No.
Dr. Pomeranz

I betcha his idea of "The Second Coming" and her version are two very different things. But, seriously...Through my many years of practice, I have come to see great validity in astrology, not only in regard to compatibility, but also as a tool for understanding life, as well as human nature.

An "astrological sign" simply means that when each one of us was born, the planets were lined up in a particular way, and the date and time we were born determines what sign we were born under. Each sign (there are 12) takes on a particular characteristic or archetype.

59

Each sign is ruled by a particular planet (there were 9, now there's 8, not counting Florida), which also has a particular energy.

Even though we are all connected and contain parts of the whole, the sign that we were born under determines our dominant personality characteristics. I know I am being general and simplistic here, especially dealing with an ancient art that dates back to 3,000 B.C. I also know that I'm not taking into account the varying aspects and degrees and transits and moons and risings and houses--(of blues, of pancakes, of leather)--that make each person's chart or roadmap unique, but let's have some fun with it anyway.

ARIES - The Ram. Ruled by the Mars Corporation - which also rules Milky Way, M&M's, Dove Bars, Starburst and Skittles (which by the way, is one of my favorite words after Spudnut and Scaloppini). Aries are full of creative energy and inspiration. They are natural born leaders--dynamic, direct, and generous. If that's not enough, Aries is also a nice, but boxy, mid-size sedan.

TAURUS - The Bull. Ruled by Venus. They are patient, persistent and never give up. They're an earth sign, so comfort and family and home are very important to them. They are loyal, grounded, stable and, like Aries, though not as sporty, the Taurus, which is primarily used by narcotic and various government agents, makes for a smooth and comfortable ride.

GEMINI - The (Olsen) Twins. Ruled by Mercury. Like their symbol, they can easily do two things at once, which can be particularly handy during love making. They are bright, friendly, mercurial, and love to talk. They could definitely use a really good calling plan with no roaming charges and free minutes after 5pm.

CANCER - The Crab. Ruled by the Moon. They are emotional, sensitive, intuitive and guided by their feelings. They love to nest and be home. They feel most secure with both HBO and the full cable package. They make great mothers, protectors and pet psychics.

LEO - The Lion. Ruled by the Sun. They are warm, loving, generous, creative and natural born leaders. They are great at being center stage and may have difficulty playing one of the elves, instead of Santa in their elementary school play.

VIRGO - The Maiden. Ruled by Mercury. They are capable, efficient, practical, sensible, and just love order. They often get a bad rap about being critical, perfectionistic, or a bit anal. But, they do make a great Oral Surgeon, Circumciser and one heck of an Accountant.

LIBRA - The Scales. Ruled by Venus. They are sociable. They seek balance and harmony. They are great lovers of beauty and comfort, but can have a weakness for anything sweet or indulgent. They also have an amazing ability to see both sides of the coin thus making them great therapists, negotiators, Haagen-Dazs and heroin addicts.

SCORPIO - The Scorpion. Ruled by Bluto (so is Popeye). They are powerful, strong willed and have extraordinary staying power. For example, here are some Scorpions: Trotsky, Indira Gandhi, Nehru, Boutros Boutros Ghali, King Hussein, Hillary Rodman Clinton, Demi-Moore, Mata-Hari and Mussolini. That about says it.

SAGITTARIUS - The Archer. Ruled by Jupiter. They are free spirits, independent, and dislike being tied down. They love to expand, explore, and have all sorts of adventures. They are the ones who sign up for those trips that offer 36 cities in just three days. They make great lovers, astronauts and lousy desk clerks at the DMV.

CAPRICORN - The Goat. Ruled by Saturn. They are hard working, diligent, determined, and practical. They are deep thinkers and are insatiable when it comes to knowledge and growth. They need purpose, love precision, and are great at completing to-do lists and ordering for the entire table at Indian and Chinese restaurants.

AQUARIUS - (when the moon. . .) The Water Bearer. Ruled by Uranus (I'm not touching that one). They are idealistic, humanitarian, artistic, unconventional, original, independent, and interested in thinking out of the box and creating new paradigms. To give you a better understanding, here are some Aquarians: Baryshnikov, Jackson Pollock, Chekhov, Darwin, Lincoln, Dostoevsky, Edison, Copernicus, Galileo and...Burt Reynolds.

PISCES - The Fishes. Ruled by Neptune. They are sensitive, romantic, intuitive, and extremely imaginative. They make great visionaries, mystics, healers, and amazing artists. So essentially, they need a manager, a wristwatch, and a very good agent.

Even though we are dealing with only Sun signs here, you can see that perhaps some signs might be more compatible and complimentary than others. Instead of trying to change the very nature of one another, it's probably much more loving and a whole lot easier to accept, respect, and value what each person has to offer. You'll have a much sweeter ride.

I will leave you with your Horoscope for the month:

Expect lots of traffic on the 110, 405, and short delays on the 118.

Your lucky numbers are: 1-900-805-5555. (Ask for Heather or Tawny.)

Flow your heart, and you will have lots of love.

Astrological information furnished by. . .

The Power of Birthdays, Stars + Numbers. - The Complete Personology Reference Guide By Saffi Crawford and Geraldine Sullivan - (a Ballantine Book, 1998).

ON RELATIONSHIPS

First, let me tell you a secret. Yes, right up front. The secret to having a wonderful, deeply satisfying, mind-altering, lip-smacking, "I can't believe how great this relationship is"—(no, it's not wearing a Zorro mask or milk chocolate underwear)—it's all you. That's right, you.

This is good news. No longer do we have to wait for someone else. Take a look at what you're bringing to all your relationships--to your partner, daughter, boss, or friend; or, if you live in California, to your high-colonic practitioner.

I can't tell you how many times I see couples, and the guy will say something like, "She never wants to have sex," or "She gained six pounds" (after their seventh child), or "I'm not attracted to her anymore." Meanwhile, he's 5' 3", balding, unshaven, weighs over 250 pounds, and wears a t-shirt that reads, "Beer Drinkers Make Better Lovers." Look at what he's offering here.

It's not just the guys. A woman in my office the other day told me, "I have no intimacy in my life." See the difference? Men: "no sex"; women: "no intimacy." I asked her to show me her appointment book. Here's a quick sampling: 6:40-6:45 - Baby and me time. 6:45-7:00 - Wake up family. Make breakfast and lunches. Sew Simba costume. 7:00-7:10 - Make beds. Clean bathrooms. Grout tile. Simonize the car. Write a fiery letter to the French Embassy.

Get my point? She has no opening, no downtime and no personal rhythm that she follows. Look at what she's bringing to her poor husband or kids, or even her dog. She's a "doing" machine. She's not present, not able to enjoy what's in front of her so that she can cultivate intimacy. When all is said and done, her headstone can read: HERE LIES SYLVIA. HER HOUSE SMELLED FRESH.

Instead of looking at the other guy, look to yourself. Are you giving your best? Is what you're offering going to create the effect you desire?

All right, let's take this even further. Look at the beliefs you bring to your relationships. Let's say you think, "People don't come through." Maybe that's been your experience, so if you unconsciously put that out, one of two things will happen. You'll either pull in people that don't come through, or you'll help disable an otherwise capable person. You see? We all comply with what's put out there. It just works that way.

Let me give an example for all of you visual folks. I'm at a party and I'm telling a story and I somehow turn my back on this woman who I don't know, pretty much dismissing her. I focus my attention solely on my friends. You don't know me, but I'm the type that rescues ants and flies and would never want to hurt anything ever, but that's my own therapy. So I'm lying in bed that night thinking, "I have to find this woman and apologize for my rudeness," and then it hits me: this woman probably walks around thinking something like, "I don't matter" or "I'm not important." I just unconsciously picked it up and started treating her that way.

Look at what you believe and are unconsciously saying. Don't feel lovable enough? Sexy enough? Good partner material? Do you think all men cheat? Are women high maintenance? Too emotional? Are your beliefs getting in the way of what you want and what is actually possible?

Next time you are at the bank or at the grocery store, look at how you are standing. What are you saying? Are you approachable and present? Or, Are you thinking about the past or the future?

You want great love or sex or work or health or money? Look to yourself.

Optional Assignment

Ask your partner and/or loved ones how they would describe you. Ask them to go beneath the surface and describe who they really believe you to be and what kind of energy you bring to them. Make it safe for them to be completely honest with you so that they may express their experience and tell you exactly how they feel. If several people say the same thing, it may be time to re-examine what you're putting out there.

Relationships are all about giving your best, or at least being honest when you can't. The worst that can happen, at least in your heart of hearts, is to know that you've given it your best shot. That's something you can feel really good about.

ON COMMUNICATION

I'm reminded of the comic strip "Cathy" that I saw years and years ago by Cathy Guisewite. I'm probably making half of it up, like when you play telephone and it starts out, "I am going to the store" and ends up, "You smell like Albacore."

So forgive me for this botch job, but it goes something like this:

In the first frame, there's a picture of Cathy sitting in a car with her boyfriend driving. There's a bubble above her head. She's thinking, "He's so quiet. I wonder why he's not talking to me? He probably doesn't love me anymore." As the frames go on, it gets worse and worse in her mind. "I'm sure it's because I'm fat." Next frame: "He's got someone else and is afraid to tell me." Next frame: "Screw him. I don't need this. I'm breaking up with him!" Finally, in the last frame, you see a bubble over *his* head, and he's thinking: "Maybe Tuesday's a good day to lube the car."

This is such a great example of how it can be out there. Trust me, it's not just a girl thing. The roles can be easily reversed, except she's probably really thinking that Condoleezza Rice makes an excellent side dish. It's also not just a boy-girl thing. Sadly, projecting and miscommunication happens all the time, like a bad 1940's movie where she reacts to something benign, he reacts to her reaction, she to his, his to hers, and before you know it she's off marrying the band leader. So here are some simple, sane, loving ways that can help us understand each other better.

A great tool for clear communication is to use a scale from 1 to 10. Ten being important, one being whatever-- let's say, what's for lunch? When one person feels something is a "10", but the other person holds it as a "2", the upset can be enormous. For example, if it's a "10" for me that the dishes are washed at night and I don't say that, and every morning I get up and there's piles of plates in the sink with little pieces of macaroni bonded to it, I'm gonna feel upset. It's not that he doesn't love me, it's just that clean dishes are a "2" to him (which is probably much healthier than my "10," but again, that's my own therapy).

Conversely, if you say it's a "10" that I kiss you on the nose or come to the party with you...if it's a "10" for you, you're kissed and I'm there.

Even if you think their "10" is silly, unless it's soul compromising, give it to them. We all have a few "10's." By the way, if you or your friends or loved ones have lots of "10's," I'll see you at my office a week from Tuesday.

This is such a simple, clean way to understand one another. It's great with kids too. If they fall down or start crying, at first everything feels like a "10." But see if they can give a number on how much it hurts. You could kiss their number down, one kiss per number. Is it a five kisser? A three? By the way, this may not be the healthiest way to go with a 50 year old, but who am I to judge?

Here is another tool for great communication. Think about what makes you feel the most loved. Really think about it. What I find is that we usually love the other guy in ways we like, but not necessarily how they like it. For instance, some people like to be touched. It makes them feel loved. If you touch them or hold their hands, they feel really cared for. I was at a party with two friends of mine who are married. They were each talking to other people. I saw my friend walk over to his wife and just touch her on the shoulder. You could see her whole body relax and melt into his hand.

Some people like to be told loving things: "I love you," "You're the best." I always thought I should make a list of all the stuff I'd like to hear and just give it to my boyfriend. Then I can yell out "#46!" and he just looks down the list and reads me #46. "Oh Susan, you have the body of an 18-year-old but the wisdom of an old soul." "#64!": "I will never find anyone like you--even after death!" "#27!": "I have never before loved a woman with such thin thighs."

Then there are those who like when people do things for them. This is actually my personal fave. If I came home and the laundry was done and my tires were rotated, I would feel completely loved. Now if my boyfriend came home and I did his laundry and rotated his tires (and what man doesn't love that), he would think it's really nice, but this would not be the way to truly love this man.

Think about it. We all like a little of everything. But think about what really makes you feel most loved. Tell your partner or your mother or your lover or your friends. "They should know" doesn't fly. Teach them how to love and care for you. Ask them. Find out what really does it for them. By the way, for those of you who love to hear it, "#23!"

Optional Assignment

Make a list of all the important things that you care about in your life. Number them (10 being most impor-

tant). First, really look at your list. Is this what you want your life to be about? Is it about dirt or abs or things? Is it about creativity or connection or being of service?

Get clear on what you're doing and what you really value. This may sound dramatic, but I sometimes ask myself if I had a year or two to live, what then would I really care about? Somehow that flat stomach drops about 10 points. If that were the case, what would you really do or say? How would you spend your day?

Now take your 10's and those things that you value that are not expressed and express them, especially to those who you live, work, or play with. Find out what's important to you, what's important to the people in your life, and what you both may not be saying. Get clear. Be deliberate. Speak your truth. Then go out there and really love each other up.

THE POWER OF NO

As I see it, there are three types of people. There are the "yes" people who feel compelled to please and say "yes" to pretty much everything asked of them, whatever the cost to themselves. They are usually the ones who order a five-year subscription to "Plumbing and Pipes" magazine so their neighbor's kid can get points for their school, invite Jehovah Witnesses into their homes for dinner and a movie, or find themselves at J.F.K. Airport at 3 a.m. looking for a friend of a friend's lost luggage, which is no big deal except for the fact that they live in Houston.

Then there are those of us who can spot the "yes" people a mile away and ask outrageous stuff from them like, "Could you go to the airport to pick up the luggage...?" or, "I'm racing in the Demolition Derby next week. Can I borrow your car?"

Finally there are those of us who are balanced, loving, generous, and have the ability to say "no." They know how to take care of themselves and others all at the same time. What is that, like about three people, including all of North and South America, the Middle East, the Ukraine, and most of Southeast Asia?

So how can you tell if you are a "yes" person? Well, take a moment and answer the following..."yes" or "no."

1. You're taking this test.

2. You're seriously considering carrying your ex-boyfriend's child because his wife doesn't want to lose her figure.

3. You find yourself hiding all the time and no longer answer the door or pick up the phone.

4. You just agreed to head the committee to raise funds for the albino sea otter, but you're already in charge of the bake sale for the V.C.F.M.--"visually challenged flying mammals" (...blind bats).

5. You just said "yes" to baby-sit for "Omen Boy" for the next 16 weeks while his parents take a cruise ship to Helsinki and can't be reached because they're in the middle of the Bering Sea.

Personally, saying "no" hasn't been easy for me. I'm not that great at it, and the times I have said "no" to someone, I wind up feeling so guilty that I usually end up buying them a car or something. Even when people work for me, I usually end up overpaying them. What? You think $140 to clean a studio apartment is too much? Or an $18 tip for one saltine and a fruit cup?

When I think back to all the people I've tried to please, or done stuff for, or acquiesced to, or didn't speak my mind to, truth is, I don't even know these people anymore. I suppressed my expression, subverted my time or energy or my heart--for what? So people would like me? To keep the peace? To be a good person? It didn't dawn on me that saying "yes" all the time had nothing to do with being a good or spiritual person. And that saying

74

"no" didn't mean I was bad or self-absorbed.

Sometimes saying "no" comes out of love. For both ourselves and for others. Don't be afraid to set boundaries. Trust me, it's healthy, and you won't be walking around resentful or compelled to eat all your kid's Halloween candy and have to replace it in the morning.

Oh yeah, don't be making up excuses why you can't say "yes." Especially if you're over 50 and probably won't remember what you said anyhow. At least if you're gonna lie, get your dates straight: the Kentucky Derby is at the beginning of May, and Mardi Gras, way before Easter. It is also best to be short. A simple "no" is fine. Not, "No, because even though I love your dog and would love to feed 'Nikita,' he almost bit my entire ear off last time and almost nicked my left testicle..."

By the way, never take charge of someone's pets-- unless it's a turtle, so that if it dies, it can easily be switched. Also, I wouldn't let anyone borrow anything, unless it's OK if you never see it again. Especially to that neighbor who borrowed your favorite sweater that now fits your kid's Barbie.

So next time when someone asks for a favor, wait the beat. Buy yourself some time and ask yourself two questions: "How would I feel about myself if I did?" and, "How would I feel about myself if I didn't?" Give generously and freely, but be the captain of your life.

Optional Assignment

Put yourself aside and say "yes" to everyone's wishes for the next three weeks. After you've given $1500 to the Policeman's Ball, gained 36 pounds from the thin mint Girl Scout Cookies or bought insurance simply because *the salesman looks so sad, do you feel that you're a better person? Look at the bright side--at least you got cookies out of the deal.*

WARM HANDS, COLD FEET

In counseling couples who are about to be married, or about to make any kind of big life commitment for that matter, I can usually tell how far off the wedding or event is...

If it's six months or more away, the love birds are myopic and totally focused on one another. They talk baby talk and have these cute little pet names for each other like Pillow Lips or Pookie Pants. Personally, I prefer food names like My Little Hostess Cupcake, Chocolate Kiss, Cherry Jubilee, Chicken Tender, Honey Bunches of Oats, or Hunky Beef Pot Pie. I would stay away from Ho Ho, Fruit Pie, Tart, Beef Jerky, Pesto, and definitely Cup-O-Noodles. Oh, and of course, don't call him Mr. Peanut, whatever you do.

Now if the wedding or commitment is less than six months away, fear can creep in and the thought of attaching more to "Pookie" can start feeling "Spooky." So, you know that little mole that used to be so endearing? It's now taken on the size of a '54 Buick. Simply put, you've become obsessed and hypercritical. Even though you intellectually know it's not the issue and it really doesn't matter, that's all you can focus on.

Rest assured, this is common. Marriage and life commitments are big steps and no matter how wonderful your beloved is, it can bring up fear and doubt. And making a mountain out of a mole (hill) can be part of it. Let's put it this way, if you find yourself annoyed with the way your partner breathes, you are definitely at this stage.

So how do we turn this around? Talk to each other. That's it. Tell each other what's on your mind and in your heart. The more you do, the lighter and closer you'll feel. Talk about your fears and concerns no matter how uncomfortable. It's a chance to move out of judgment and isolation towards real intimacy.

Talk about everything under the sun: your pictures, experiences, and expectations. Explore choice, freedom, and the very nature of fear and doubt. Truly, to question is a healthy thing.

Still not sure if it's the jitters or if you're seeing *real* red flags? Well, yes, sometimes we are so smitten or focused on the wedding or the move or the next step that we don't have the objectivity to see what's really going on. So stepping back can be an important part of the process.

Here are some red flags you might want to watch out for: he insists you use coasters - even at the ball park; he writes memos while making love; calls you "mommy" or needs you to cut his meat. She yells "Bubba" during sex, but your name is really "Norman"; has eaten only two rice cakes since Labor Day 2000; gets Valentine's and "thank you" notes from the entire 7th Fleet.

Talk about red flags, I once had a patient who wanted to get married and create a close, loving family, but like so many of us, she was loving the chemical rush and ignored the truth about her partner and married him. This man had a dog who was neutered, a cat that was neutered, and he had a vasectomy. So I guess *he* was neutered. Not only that, this guy lived on Cemetery Lane, and the day she moved in with him, there was a Transylvania-like storm and a power outage. Oh yeah, that was *after* the electrical fire. So pretty much the only thing missing was flying monkeys and "Surrender Dorothy" written in the sky. If there are red flags, better to confront them now than eight years later.

But if it is warm hands, cold feet, make sure it's safe for both of you. Fear can be a natural reaction to the unknown. There's no need to personalize, react, or defend it. Hold it loosely. There's a world of difference between relating to our fears, as opposed to reacting from our fears. One brings us closer, the other pushes love away.

One last thing. What's beyond all the fear is an opportunity to jump out of our chattering minds and into the unlimited celebration of our hearts. And this is a very good thing.

Optional Assignment

Pick something that you want to do in life but are afraid to do—assuming that it is both ethical and safe for you and for others.

1. *Write down what would happen if you went ahead.*

2. *Write what would happen if you didn't.*

Now answer this question: What choice makes you feel best about yourself?

THE ART OF
LIVING TOGETHER

I can actually tell how long a couple has been living together by what they wear around the house. In the beginning, couples start out wearing hardly any clothes. What they do wear is playful or see-through, so they can have easy access to one another.

Shortly after that come the socks. It starts out innocently enough. The place is drafty, you feel a chill. No big deal, still fine. Naked and socks, eyeglasses and socks, even underwear and socks (the good kind you just bought, not the ones your mother bought for you 13 years ago, but the kind that still has it's elastic). Soon comes the t-shirts--still good. Thought out. Matches the new pants. She wears his shirt; he's got new shorts. Same category, still sexy.

Now we start a little shift here. He means no harm. But now he's wearing the same day t-shirt for the night t-shirt. O.K. You love him. He smells good to you but somehow the shirts start changing: old 5K shirts, Laker shirts (or for her, aerobic cat shirts). Still fine, but it doesn't stop here. Now you're sleeping with METALLICA or "Just Say Moe" or even worse, the "I like Cheese" shirt his Mother brought back from her trip to Switzerland and other neutral countries. In other words, his old stash: the stained ones with entire sleeves missing. So now you've got the socks, the old t-shirt but still, the good underwear.

Now winter is coming so you bring out the sweat-shirts, followed by the sweatpants. So now you have the sweatshirt, sweatpants, cheese t-shirt, no longer the good underwear, and of course, the socks.

So these are pretty much your outfits. You hadn't planned it, but these are pretty much it. Then something good happens. Over the years, your outfits become see-through again, only this time it's from too much washing. But it's nice. It's nice to see each other again.

Now, remember in the beginning you'd watch any-thing on television just to be with your loved one? Let's put it this way, I know more about Stalin than I do about my entire family. Things change. My boyfriend's attention span for Debbie Travis' "Painted House" is waning and the second I leave the room, even for two seconds—BAM!--on goes the Hitler Channel. He thinks I don't know. Hell, the whole neighborhood knows. (Muffling the sound of marching Nazi's is not an easy thing to do.)

Another thing that changes when you are living to-gether is the shaving schedule, where in the beginning you shave constantly. You want to be at your best and ready at all times. Then it starts changing. You miss a day here, a day there. It becomes calculated. You figure you're not gonna see a lot of action on Easter or Yom Kippur. Confirmations and circumcisions? Definitely out. So why bother? Then you settle into a new schedule that works for both of you. You make a deal: we shave only in the months that start with a vowel.

Then there's the hand signals... You know when someone calls and your beloved picks up the phone and you signal to him that you don't want to talk. In the begin-ning, you are new. He doesn't fully understand the new system. You look like you are either landing a 747 at LAX or you're some kind of psychotic referee at a sporting

82

event. "She's taxiing...no she's traveling...she's traveling in a taxi! That's it...she's out. She's out traveling in a taxi...but she's safe. Yesiree, don't worry, she is definitely safe."

In time things really start clicking, like a well-oiled machine. You can actually look at each other and communicate just about anything without moving any organ below your neck. Just by using your mouth and your eyebrows, you can tell each other anything: when it's time to go, if toilet paper is stuck to your shoe, if you've got a noodle on the side of your mouth. If you're *really* good, not only do you know you've got food in your teeth, but you also know what kind and which teeth.

Besides providing great comedy material, living together is an art form. The secret of a great relationship is to be and give your best. That's it. Show up and give it the best you've got. Sounds easy enough. right?

So what happens? Well, balancing a relationship with your self and your partner, and the rest of your life, isn't so easy. It's real easy to get into the "doing" mode, losing sight of what really matters to you. The key is to stay conscious. To feed yourself so you're centered and grounded. Let's face it. Life can be a rocky ride--all the more reason to feed your soul. You can't have good relationships if you show up empty.

Optional Assignment

Find out what gets you right. Be still. Listen... Do anything that you can do that pops you out of your routine and reminds you of the real deal.

So here it is. You want a great relationship?
Make yourself great.

MANLY MEN

Years ago, I had all these wonderful male clients. It occurred to me that no matter what their issue was, they were all having the same underlying experience. They all felt isolated and painfully disconnected from themselves and others.

Now I'm not saying that women don't share this experience, but somehow women have more permission in our society to feel and express their emotions-- to touch and enjoy greater intimacy. My boyfriend is always amazed at how quickly women bond with one another. Pretty much all it takes is one trip to the bathroom together, and we know who we love and loved and why, how much sex we're having and why, our menstrual histories, and where we stand on circumcision.

Guys, on the other hand, are very good at all sorts of stats and state capitals.

It quickly became clear to me that if these guys were open to being in a group, they could move out of isolation and really start to fly. I was so pleased when they all said they'd give it a try, and I set out to find a great male therapist for them. When they all said, "No, you lead the group," I thought, "cool," and that's how I started running men's groups.

I was blown away by all the stuff men think they're supposed to be. Instead of being taught to embrace all parts of themselves, they have repeatedly been pro-grammed that it's not "manly" to show any kind of sensi-tivity, neediness, uncertainty, softness, or to like Barbara Streisand (especially the "Funny Girl" years). No wonder these sweet men felt so cut off. Living in a box is unnatu-ral. It's painful. It was preventing them from experiencing themselves as balanced people.

I was also amazed at what men thought women wanted. For instance, we needed them to perform and be hard at all times. Give me a break. After the initial six months, we'd much rather watch "Sex in the City" than actually have it.

Conversely, I was so relieved to find that not all these men needed women to weigh 82 pounds (that's during pregnancy). I also found after a certain age (35-ish), that along with the visual, men really wanted a full experience with a partner, someone to sleep with, really talk with, laugh with, and, yes, even eat with (preferably more than two leaves of lettuce with dressing on the side).

In truth, I probably learned more from them than they from me.

What makes someone "manly" or "sexy" anyhow? It's subjective. People respond to all kinds of things. There is one thing, however, most women agree on that is not so sexy: the toupee, especially if you're going for that Don King or Kramer look. Also, it scares us when it moves.

Personally, I've made it a rule never to date anyone prettier or thinner than myself. It's incredible to me how we're all subliminally duped into perpetuating myths about men. Ask pretty much anyone these days who is a "manly man," and you'd probably hear names like, Rocky, Clint, Sean Connery, George Clooney, Rosemary Clooney, Arnold, etc. What is that? My guess is they all appeal to our need to either be protected or be the protector. But that's a whole other story. Call me crazy, but I don't think you'll find Rabbi Schneerman or Gandhi's name on anyone's "sexiest man" list, or any spiritual person for that matter. I can just hear it now... "Oh, Deepak." "Ooo, shake it Ramthra."

Anyhow, I just loved watching these men as they started to explore and allow for different parts of themselves to emerge. I loved watching as they began to come from a place of tenderness with themselves and one another. At first, if there was any kind of emotional or physical intimacy in the room, they could only handle it in small doses, and usually stopped it by punching each other in the arm or something. It was very funny. But then when they exhaled into a full range of feelings, it was nothing short of exquisite. They could be assertive and receptive, exertive and still--the Yin and the Yang. Very beautiful stuff.

This is true for all of us. Peace lies in honoring all the aspects that make us who and what we are. It's not important that we define energy as either masculine or feminine, but what is important is that we integrate and embrace that energy in becoming what we truly are: whole human beings.

Optional Assignment

Make a pie chart. Remember those? Look to see where your energy is really going. Too much activity? Not enough? Putting out too much? Not getting enough back? Having any fun? Now's the time to take a look. Make a second pie chart. How would you like it to be? Put your considerations to the side and just go for it. Pretend that we're not only allowed to, but are supposed to create any kind of life we want. Just pretend. What do you think? What's it going to be?

VENUS ENVY

This will probably get me in a lot of trouble. But please, guys, do you really think you're doing a great job out there? I love men. I really do. Truly, I've been blessed. For there are many wonderful men all around me, but look at the state this planet is in.

Please, if you think it's about who's got the bigger nuclear device at this point, I don't think so. This is not gym class and it's getting us nowhere, except maybe dead. Pakistan has one, Iran wants one, and Korea wants a bigger one. Come on, we don't care about the size of your missile, we never did. We want intimacy, connection. The focus is all wrong. Forget the bombs. Forget the oil. There's a hole in the ozone layer the size of Pluto and we can now get a tan at four in the morning. People are starving, homeless, and sick. Come on, the 3R's are now Rap, Ritalin, and Reality TV.

Is it all men's fault? Of course not. We all allowed this, but the killing and destroying has got to stop. Please don't misunderstand me. There have been many great men out there: Lincoln, Churchill, Roosevelt, Margaret Thatcher, Wally Amos, Martin Sheen, but look at the truth of things.

I think it's time to put the guns down. It's women's turn. We are just different and so are our priorities. I don't know if we're socialized into it or not, but we do come from a different mindset. This is interesting. I saw this very cool video where there were three boys and three girls around ages four and five. Each child was given a videocassette to play with. Within minutes the boys were holding the cassettes like guns, shooting the crap out of each other, while the girls were gathered together holding onto the things like little mothers embracing their children.

Come on, surely this world would have better health care and child care and elder care. There would certainly be more intimacy, mutual cooperation, and a deeper relationship to the environment. Besides free tampons and chocolate, things would run *way* more efficiently.

Let's face it: we do most of the work anyhow. This issue comes up in my office all the time. She gets up at Zero Dark Thirty, gets the kids up, washes them, dresses them, gets the breakfast foods together and the lunches, slaps some clothes on, usually rushing, gets the kids to school--usually different ones--pumps some gas, makes it to work, works, does some errands at lunch, works some more, picks up the kids, banks, shops, rushes home, straightens up while cooking the dinner and making play dates and studying for the bar or a social work exam, serves the dinner, cleans up, helps with homework and the washing of the kids, puts them to sleep with stories or songs, falls into bed and...he wants Sex!?

Is this just in America? Oh no, I'll never forget this image. I was on a bus in India looking out the window. I saw women dressed in beautiful Saris hoeing the fields in the hot sun. This one woman was hoeing with one hand and holding a suckling baby with another, smiling and carrying on a conversation with her other Sari friends while across the field in the shade were these two guys smoking, squatting, spitting, drinking, and playing cards.

Guys, it's time to step down. You can eat your Honey Nuts and watch the Laker playoffs. With the exception of

90

opening a few jars now and then, the day is yours. You can build and fix and destroy stuff to your heart's content. Really, this works for us too. Personally, I always thought that without men in charge there'd be a whole lot of fat happy women running around. So go ahead. Feel free to pursue your dreams. Find some balance. It's a good deal. Let *us* take over for a while.

Here are just a few of the changes we could look forward to if women ruled the world:

- Weapons, nuclear arsenals, and "The 3 Stooges" would be banned.

- Every 28 days you get to lie in bed.

- Also, free Hostess Happy Cakes every 28 days.

- Egg shaped pastel-colored cars.

- H.G.T.V. and the Food Channel moves to Prime Time.

- Less ESPN and the Hitler Channel.

- Cary Grant movies 24/ 7.

- More touching, less sex.

- Unlimited cell phone and rollover minutes.

- No Paintball.

- Wrestling? I don't think so.

- Bendy heated speculums.

- And of course, no Hummers.

OK, maybe I've been a lot lopsided about all of this, so let me mention what's really great about men. They're much lighter than us. Truly. Here's a fine little example. I'm at the gym and listening to these guys play racquet ball. While they're slamming this ball around, they're yelling back and forth things like, "You stink," "F-you," "Move your fat A," and at the end they say to each other, "Great game--let's go for a beer!"

Now, you say just one of those things to a woman and we won't talk to you for 11 years. We personalize everything. Guys are generally stronger and taller and can protect and lift and reach stuff. They go deep, not wide, and have incredible concentration. They have fun and are funny and sweet and snorey and some even smell good (my boyfriend smells like chocolate chip cookies). It's also OK to get them wet.

The truth is, individually, men are great. It's the collective testosterone energy--(sounds like it could be something from Ronzoni—"Ronzoni's Testosteroni")--that's getting out of hand.

This is written in the spirit of fun. The real truth is both men and women are able to be mindful, soulful, empathetic, powerful and cooperative. It's about being balanced. It's about being loving. It's about being more conscious.

Optional Assignment

For the next week, do one thing each day that makes the planet better. It doesn't have to be big. You don't have to cure AID's (you can if you want).

For example, pick up a piece of trash.

Be nicer on the road.

Give a compliment or your time or your money.

Allow someone to give to you.

Help someone. In some cases, stop helping someone.

Just keep in mind the greater good. If enough of us looked at the big picture and took action, the change would be revolutionary. It would uplift the human race.

OUR KIDS

I have this sweet client. I'll call her "Tiffani." She's every man's fantasy in her cute little Catholic school uniform, short plaid skirt, knee socks, and bouncy blond pony tail. She has no idea she's centerfold material and that the men in my waiting room are more cleaned up each week because of her--all shaved and smelling of manly cologne. She's really been good for morale.

But here's the real deal about Tiffani: she's miserable. She's so stressed out from the demands of life--some real, some self-imposed--that at age 15 she can barely eat or sleep, and when asked about the last time she felt joy or happiness, or even really laughed hard, she talked about eating "S'mores" at some campout *six* years ago.

Why is she so stressed out? Well, let's put it this way, besides being pressured to get all A's and tote around a book bag that weighs more than a '64 Chevy (filled with books, laptop, ipod, cell, sports equipment, and various musical instruments), she has been in honor classes since preschool, lives half the week with Mom, half with Dad, has two genius brothers (you know, the kind that entered med school at ages 6 and 14), has four hours of homework each night, and to top that off, lives in L.A. where eight year olds are on the Zone Diet and the rest of them pop Skittles and take Ritalin. (How about *Skitta-lins*, fruity chewy for kids on the go!?).

It took a full week to figure out when she could even come to an appointment. Let's see...between track practice and acting class? No. Karate and ballet?... What happened? When did life get so nuts?

Tiffani is just one of the many kids I see who are pressured to take Ritalin or Adderal for their A.D.D. or A.D.H.D., so they can score higher on their S.A.T.'s and A.C.T.'s and keep up with their A.P. classes so their G.P.A.'s can get them into schools like N.Y.U. and M.I.T. Where's the joy? Where's the fun? What happened to childhood?

When Tiffani comes into my room, we talk about food--all the food she can't eat. Besides being a vegetarian--(she's so anemic, she'd be safe at a Vampire Convention)--she knows more about calories, carbs, and fats than a third year medical student.

Truth is, she loves to eat and loves to cook. She loves colors and smells and textures and tastes. She loves TV, nature, and quiet. She waits all week for Sundays when she's allowed to watch one hour of Tivo-ed TV, and is looking forward not to her Birthday or X-mas or summer, but to 2009 when she'll have time to sleep, paint, and read something not on her reading list. Come on! We've got to help these kids.

So this is what I'm thinking. Let's nix the expectations and the super-achiever mentality and nourish our children in ways that support who they are. In an attempt to open our children up to experiences and limitless opportunities, look how it can sometimes backfire by causing burnout, stress, and anxiety. Is attending a high ranking school really the only way to succeed in life? Let's help our children define themselves through their character, their quest for knowledge and passion for life, instead of their ability to ace the chemistry or college entrance exam.

We love our kids. Let's make learning and living useful, balanced, fun and most of all, meaningful. Oh, and by the way, Tiffani is now almost 16. Each day she looks for what's right about herself and her world. She is more relaxed and graceful. She cut out track, karate, and ballet. She dances with her friends instead. She's better at listening to and honoring herself and the signals of her body. She now has the ability to see what in the long run is really important (a skill I learned last Thursday). She gets mostly A's and B's (she got a "C" and didn't die), cooks up a storm, takes Friday nights and Sundays off and wears green-and-white polka dot sneakers. After all, it is her school colors.

Optional Assignment

Sit down with your child(ren) with paper and crayons or colored markers. Ask <u>them</u> to draw a pie chart showing what <u>their</u> world is like-- i.e., school, sleep, homework, volleyball, soccer, etc.

See if you can jump into their shoes and really feel what each day is like for them. Now, given the reality, like they still have to go to school, have them draw another chart. This time showing how they would like it to be--i.e., more time with friends or with you., etc. Put the two charts side by side and take time to look at it. Also look to see if you have any expectations or feelings about it all.

Together, see what you can both do to create more balance, more love and esteem, and most of all, more joy. Now do this for yourself.

McPAT

Pat is ten. The sweetest face you've ever seen. Pink cheeks. Smiley eyes. I fell in love the second I laid eyes on him. Oh yeah, Pat also stands 4'9"and weighs close to 140 lbs. Here's the deal with Pat: food has become his comfort, his fun, his hobby and his friend.

Now, Pat's parents are nice enough people and, like most parents, they truly want the best for their child. But between two full-time jobs and three other children, Pat is pretty much left alone to do and eat whatever and whenever he wants.

Here are the things that Pat loves and in the correct order: cheese sticks, corn dogs, Doritos, "chocolate any-thing," tacos, pizza, soda, crisscut fries, pies, anything fried, TV, computer, his play station, oh, and his parents. He has no close friends except in cyberspace. He is shy and sensitive and ridiculed at school. By the way, if you're gonna name your kid Pat or any other name that rhymes with fat, please don't stuff them. They're just asking for it. Same goes with Shelley ("Belly," "Smelly") or anything that ends in I-C-K or U-C-K for that matter.

Pat's room is filled with various plastic and furry toys from gazillions of McHappy meals. He knows the entire menu at Taco Bell, Carl's Jr., In-N-Out and Burger King. In geography, he can't name many of the states but he totally knows all about the Western Bacon Cheeseburger and that it goes for only $3.99. In math, he's not great with fractions and wholes and quarters but he is masterful at discerning between the 18, 24 or the 32 oz. Big Slurpee Gulp or the Mega Mountain Dew (Mountain Dew, ever drink one of those? WHOA. What the heck is in that stuff anyway, crystal meth?).

He knows all 31 flavors but can barely name any of our Presidents except for President McFlurry (he was after Cleveland and before Roosevelt, wasn't he?). He also can't spell for beans—"beenz," "beens"—but, like Pat says, "there's always spell check."

Truth is, I see several kids like Pat these days and I don't ever remember there being so many obese children. Now, don't get me wrong, I had my share of soda and carbs and sugars growing up. I used to start my day with 87 pancakes drenched in maple syrup and eight sticks of butter. By the time I got on the bus to school, I was either in a coma or frantically visiting and bouncing from seat to seat (my report card once said I was a very friendly person).

In those days, there was no such thing as A.D.D. or any correlation made between the 20 bowls of Kellogg's Sugar Smacks I ate each morning (Smack: a tip off right there) with the fact that I could not stop running and jumping and laughing (or talking for that matter). But somehow between the Mac and Cheese and the mashed potatoes, we were all out running around, riding bikes or building stuff.

We all ate together, lots of times played together, we even watched TV together. Our fast foods, like chicken pot pies, were still wholesome enough. Today, there's more sodium in one of those things than they used to embalm both Chairman Mao and Vladimir Lenin. But that was then and this is now.

Here's the deal: McPat is suffering. Let's feed him in other ways and let's offer up to our kids something better than Count Choc-u-la, Chocolate Eggos or the Steak and Egg Burrito with Coke (only $ 2.99) to start the day. Let's table the TV, the microwave and our computers and engage our children in activity and real life. Cook with them. Get them into colors and smells and energy in food--make it fun. Teach them. Have them plant stuff. Have food ready for them. They can grab some cherries or frozen grapes or juice pops as easily as the cherry-flavored Kool-Aid and the 98-lb. bag of peanut M&M's.

It's not about imposing severe restrictions on our children. That will only backfire. Again, the more you can't have, the more you must have. Having treats are fine. It is about getting them into relationship to their food and to their bodies. It's also about teaching them to self-soothe and self-regulate. Children are hungry for more than food. Let's get them emotionally and intellectually fed and excited and involved in the world.

I swear, what timing, I just got this in the mail. Now there's a thing called a Laptop Meal for kids so they literally don't have to leave their computers at all. Also, for this week only, the 800-piece Holiday Bucket at K.F.C. is now only $147.99. Heck, my tires cost less than that.

Optional Assignment

Here's a little quiz:
Say the first thing that comes to mind.

Hot _____
Winnie the _____
Big _____

101

Mr. _____

Mrs. _____

If you said Pockets, Pooh Ravioli, Mac, Peanut or Fields, or if you've just finished a Hungry man XXL Beef Steak in bourbon sauce (heck, why not get drunk too), it may be time to rethink your life and not be a slave to your fork and your knife.

THE TRUTH ABOUT LIES

Do I look fat? Don't you think my child is the most amazing kid on the planet? Was this the best sex you ever had? Do you love me as much as I love you? Let's talk about lying.

Well, as I see it, there are all kinds of lies. Little white ones where we lie to make others feel good about themselves: "You sell insurance, oh how fascinating." We lie to get out of stuff: "I'd love to come to little Aarons' soccer game on my one and only day off this month but darn, I just might be going to Bangkok for the day." Just a quick aside: you don't want to use the lines, "I have the mumps" or "My Grandmother just died," because you might end up with glands the size of Tokyo, or if Granny kicks, deep down, you're gonna feel really really bad.

All in all, these lies seem harmless enough. Then there's the bigger white lie, but still in the same category, like lies you would tell a new mother: "Trust me, in time the head will grow into his ears." Now you're not really sure about this, but why not spread a little cheer instead of instilling fear in this poor woman who just went through 52 hours of labor and whose offspring looks like a cross between Dumbo and a soft boiled egg?

Personally, I'm a terrible liar. Not that I don't lie, but I'm much better on the phone. In person, I usually blow it. I can say, "I really mean it" or "This is the truth," but somewhere in there my body stops going with the program and I'll start shaking my head "no." The truth is that I usually get busted, like the time I entered a cake in a bake contest at school and forgot to scrape off the Sarah Lee insignia imprinted from the tin on the bottom.

The stakes get a little higher when your lies could actually get you in a bit of trouble, especially if you're claiming extra dependents on your income tax and those dependents happen to be your turtle Pokey, and Sammy Davis, your one-eyed miniature chihuahua.

Now this is a broad category and like the marijuana cigarette, once you cross the line it gets easier and easier to do, escalating and leading to bigger and bigger lies. Soon you find yourself lying about almost everything until you reach what one might call the "O.J. of lies," where you actually truly believe your own fabrications. When I was younger, I told everyone I went to Woodstock. I thought it made me seem really cool. I'd meet someone and say, "Hi, I went to Woodstock." I thought I'd really impress 'em. Once someone actually said to me that they saw me in the movie, "Woodstock," and I got really excited to hear that. I had told the story so many times, I forgot I wasn't even there.

What makes us lie? We lie for tons of reasons: to stroke our egos, to make others feel good about themselves, to avoid embarrassment or punishment, or to get what we want. Parents lie, governments lie, we teach our children to lie. We lie to our bosses, our spouses, our friends, our lovers, our teachers. We lie by being silent. We think we are lying to others, but really we are lying to ourselves. The sickness we experience both inside ourselves and throughout our planet is symptomatic of the duplicity in the way we act and live.

What is lying? It's subjective. It's an ethical issue. It's between you and you. It's the difference between looking down at your shoes or the ability to look people squarely in the eye. When faced with what to say or how to handle a situation, I look at what makes me feel best about myself. It's plain and simple. It changes as I change. I used to lie constantly. Now I lie less constantly. My hope is the more conscious I become, the cleaner and more joyful my life and relationships will get.

A lot of my work with patients boils down to whether or not a person comes from a place of integrity. What they usually find is the more ethical they become, the easier their lives get. In essence, we start to heal when we start to get real.

Now this is not a new concept. For instance, in 12-Step Programs part of the healing process is about taking responsibility for all the ca-ca in the past, such as personal inventories and making amends whenever possible. Jews have Yom Kippur, the Day of Atonement, asking God for forgiveness. Native Americans confess their sins to shamans, Christians to priests, Buddhists have Karma. It goes on and on.

People seek therapists and doctors in an attempt to clean up their acts. It sure looks to me like we have a great need to transcend duplicity. Do you lie on a resume so you can get a better job? Do you lie about your age or weight or ability or social status? Would you lie to protect someone from physical or emotional pain? Where would you draw the line?

Here's the deal. There's a lot of lying going on about things that don't need to be lied about. Let's not accept this as our lot. We certainly have the power to alter the amount of deception in our lives. I'm thinking it's time to get honest. Look at the ripple effect it could have. Does this mean blurting out your truth everywhere you go? I hope not. Let's ask ourselves better questions. Is it kind?

What will the information do? Is it useful? And the mother of all questions: What is really the truth?

I'd like to leave you with two questions: 1. Do these pants make me look fat? And, 2. Did you lose weight?

Optional Assignment

See if you can go through one day without lying to yourself and to others. I'm on my sixth try--oops, now I have to start all over again.

ON DIVORCE OR MOVING ON

A beautiful part of the work I do is that I get to see patterns. Nothing or no one is isolated. Like nature, things ebb and flow and people seem to go through similar things at the same time. Besides the obvious patterns like being overbooked in January after the New Year's resolutions, and in the fall when the kiddies are back in school, I'm also booked when the seasons change.

Some people seem to come alive when it's hot and bright and steamy (that's how I like my men, and my vegetables, for that matter) and tend to prune up in the winter months. Some thrive when it gets cold and dark and moody (some like their partners that way, but that's a whole other story). These people usually love Miles Davis and look great in scarves and sweaters and even ski apparel.

There are times where most everyone I see feels restless or can't sleep, perhaps due to some collective event that's happened, like 9/11, or about to happen, like before an earthquake. Things come in cycles. All of a sudden I'll get tons of calls and everyone is depressed or anxious or using (drugs, alcohol, cookie dough, etc.). It's amazing to witness.

Right now it's summer, and my office is filled with people who are either looking at, or deciding to break up their relationships. Now this rarely happens in November and December. Even if you can't stomach the person you're with, from mid-October until that ball goes down on New Year's Eve, odds are no one's going anywhere.

Sometimes divorce is appropriate. There's nothing sadder than two people living vacantly and just going through the motions. I always thought people should renew their vows often. You get to look at how you're really doing. It keeps the relationship fresh and alive, offering us an opportunity to celebrate our union again and again.

Some people are blessed and get a lifetime with one another. For others, it's a shorter run. But the truth is, when a relationship is over, it's over. Now I'm not advocating divorce just because you hit a snag with each other. Far from it. Always, always give it your best shot, because our partners and relationships can be our biggest teachers. If we can stay conscious, relationships can provide the context to heal almost anything. By allowing ourselves to be intimately known, we open the door to a more deeply lived life. Isn't that what love is really about? The goodies are never-ending.

But here's the deal. If each of you is giving your best and you've tried everything to save your relationship, but you're growing east and your beloved is growing west, it may be time to let each other go. Some signs of this are: say you've stopped eating meat and wearing leather and your idea of nirvana is meditation, and blowing it out is nude dancing on the summer solstice, and your partner smells of venison and their idea of "Nirvana" is the band, and blowing it out to them is nude bowling on Wednesday nights at the all-you-can-eat Bowl-A-Rama... Well, call me crazy, but it might be time to reconsider the deal. All kidding aside, there are times when releasing each other can be for the greater good.

Sometimes people stay way too long or they leave their relationships only to do the same thing again and again.

Personally, I hold the record for this last one. It took me a few tries to finally get it right. Now I'm not gonna tell how many times I've been married but let's put it this way, if I melted down all my wedding rings, I'd have enough gold to buy a quaint B&B in Carmel and a small third-world country. By the way, if you need any toaster ovens, blenders or seal-a-meals, I'm sure I could cut you a good deal.

Now I know divorce is not for everyone. But if you find yourself staying because the thought of being alone is terrifying, or if you're taking Prozac as the only way to be in this thing, or if the names Ben and Jerry or Sarah Lee gets you more excited than the person you said "I did" with, then we need to talk. Trust me, it's a zillion times more painful to live in this soul-compromising state than the perceived pain and fear of the unknown. Again, as a culture we are addicted to getting sustenance and meaning from "out there." We're not taught to look inside and just be at peace within ourselves and in life as it is, with or without partners.

Is it better to be the leaver or the leavee (sounds like one of the twelve tribes of Israel)? Well, no one likes to be left. Even if breaking up is a great idea and you were thinking about it yourself, if they said it first, your ego goes nuts. Unless you're really secure (at last count I think there were fourteen of you), your ego takes a beating. Now about the leaver, if you're an alien or sociopath or from a Nordic country, you're OK. If you're Catholic, Jewish, Italian, Greek, Middle Eastern, Mediterranean, or from Florida and you've been taught that guilt is one of the five major food groups, it's no picnic either. The truth is, we're not taught it's OK to move on, or that letting go can be an exquisite act of love.

Divorce can be rough. At first you can't eat, you can't sleep. But the truth is, you never looked better and this feeds a sick part of you. You're losing weight. You're looking great. Who cares that you could pass out at any moment and that your nerves are so shot that you're crying at Hallmark and Forest Lawn commercials. You're looking hot. So a part of you gets into it and hopes that you bump into your ex-beloved so that they can see what a big fat mistake they made. But you know what happens. That one morning when you wake up all wrong and you look like the puffy Elvis and your hair looks like a science fair project...That's when you bump into them. It always happens that way. Always.

One last thing, divorce can be a delicate time, especially if there are children. So be kind. Be kind and generous, so when you look back you can be proud of yourself. Don't get caught up in who gets what. In the long run, leaving with compassion and dignity is way better than leaving with the good dishes and the DVD player. Even if it's got surround sound.

PART III.
THE ESSENTIALS

ON FOOD

When it comes to food there are two different types of people. There are those of us who actually take one scoop of ice cream with the correct utensil, put it in a bowl, bring it to the table and wait until it's melted to just the right room temperature. Then there's the rest of us who eat it out of the carton standing up still holding our car keys, either bending spoons right and left, or using some kind of power tool like a drill or a Sears circular saw, because it's frozen solid.

There is no in-between here. If you forget to eat, have Halloween candy left in December, and have no idea how many calories or points or fat grams are in a package of string cheese, then you are part of a select group. You are spared the insanity that goes on in the minds of the rest of us who never bake, but just eat cookie dough and have sex to burn off dinner.

I am from an ethnic background. (I don't want to say which one, but it rhymes with "blueish.") For us, food was a part of everything. Same with Italians, Greeks, and most Middle Eastern cultures. Let's put it this way, those thin little wafers my Catholic friends got at Mass each week would never fly in my family. When I was young, I associated everything with food. Name a place: The beach...ice cream with sand in it. The ball park...hot dogs, of course. Heck, the real reason I went to temple

113

all those years was for the whitefish and the marble cake. Then there are the holidays: chocolate Santas and dreidels and bunnies. Even Passover...heaven forbid us blueish people could go eight days without chocolate covering our matzoh.

You get the point. Food and cooking and smells were a way of life: safe, comforting, festive, home. No matter where you've come from, here we all are in a society of mixed messages saying that eating is bad and thin is good. You must have buns of steel and six-pack abs, even if it's genetically not in your cards and your ancestors are naturally curvy.

In our culture we are either told, or it is implied, that if our bodies don't fit the standard one-dimensional mold, then there must be something wrong with us and therefore we have no self control. Is this nuts or what? All this is a breeding ground for self-rejection, which leads us into cycles of senseless starvation, deprivation, and, ultimately, overeating.

Our constant monitoring has turned us into crazy people looking at what we should or shouldn't eat. We define ourselves by our food. "Were we bad today?" "Were we good?" Is this what we want to be doing? Diets are unnatural. They imply that we are not self-regulating. They keep us from the intimacy of listening to our own rhythms and hungers. By incessant dieting we give up our power and the opportunity to learn how to really and truly nourish ourselves.

How can we get out of this mess? How do we stand up and take back the joy of our own yearnings and our own bodies?

Be in the present and listen. That's it, just listen. Listen to what your being tells you. Is it even food you need? What are you *really* hungry for? Are you hungry for parts of yourself that are not expressed? Are you hungry to create? Do you need comfort or safety or soothing or fun? Do you need to physically move or dance or sleep? Are you using food as company, as a friend, or as a lover? Are you giving yourself what you need?

If you are hungry for food, are you giving yourself what you need physically? Look to see what it is your body really wants. You might be surprised how easy food gets when you finally give your body that carb or oil you've been depriving it of. Real power and self love comes from honoring the messages that you get, no matter what anybody or anything outside of yourself says. So take back your body and your life, and live full out!

Optional Assignment

On a scale from 1-10, 1 being starved, 10 being stuffed, how physically hungry are you? Try not to get to a 1 or a 2, because you are bound to eat anything. Even the goldfish isn't safe. If you are a 3 or 4, ask yourself what is it that my body really needs? Do I need water? Crave greens or fruit? Do I want something hot or cold or room temperature? Crunchy, chewy, soothing, salty, sour, sweet...Make sure this one comes from body hunger. (If you think you need a Hostess Fruit Pie, it's from your head).

Keep asking questions. Some of you may become so finely tuned that you'll actually intuit what color or colors your body might need, and how much you need.

Just take notice. Practice listening to the messages you are getting. For now, take all judgments away. Just see what comes up. Even if you get 8 avocados, you might need the oil. Maybe you get oatmeal and meat; you might need the fiber or the protein. If you keep getting animal protein and you've been a vegetarian since the government declared ketchup a vegetable, you might want to reconsider.

Unless there is a medical or spiritual reason, I suggest that you start to honor these messages. If you eat from this place of listening you will never be overweight or underweight. You'll feel less crazy and won't feel compelled to justify to the checker the reason you're buying the 88-pound box of Whitman Samplers and the 36-gallon bottle of Diet Coke.

ON EXERCISE

Well, "exercise" means different things to different people. For instance, there are those of us who don't like to sweat. These are the people that think that flossing, when done properly, can be downright exhausting. These are also the people that carbo-load before a miniature golf game, which I can totally understand. Getting that pimply ball through the clown head without hitting a tonsil isn't as easy as it looks.

Then there are those of us who exercise moderately. They know how to self-regulate. They know when they're full and when it's time to stop. Personally, I don't know any of these people, but I did have a friend who had a friend whose cousin went to religious school with one. Anyhow, these are the people that sweat correctly, like in between their cleavage, or display just a hint of moisture on their upper lip, unlike the rest of us who look like we made in our pants.

There are those of us who exercise like Marines from January 1st thru January 4th, the day after Thanksgiving, and after milestone birthdays that end in 0. These people do most things that way. They start out unbelievably strong. They lift weights the size of Rhode Island, and run 18 miles in the sand listening to the group Megadeath coming out of their fanny packs. They're all cow, no carbs. They're usually the ones that grunt while lifting like

117

they're in some kind of gym porno. Unfortunately, these people usually end up with a strained or ruptured spleen or a herniated heinie. (By the way, the first 5 days of a relationship with these people are to die for!).

Then there are those of us who are hardcore addicts. If these people don't sweat, it can get nasty. How can you tell if you are one of these people? Well, if you find yourself getting really agitated because you had to shorten your daily 16 mile run or 55 mile bike ride because of your own wedding, most likely, you are one of them. Or, if you show up to Granny's funeral in your sweat pants or jog bra and keep looking at the second hand or your L.E.D. digital stop watch, then yep, it's you.

By now we all know the benefits of regular exercise. It improves heart function, the intake of oxygen, lowers blood pressure, controls weight, tones and builds muscles--the goodies are endless. Psychologically, exercise relieves stress, gives us an overall feeling of well being, and tends to quiet the chatter of our restless minds. Not bad.

But before we talk about deciding what kind of exercise is right for you and how to gracefully integrate it into your life, let's talk about the attitude and all the cool gear that goes with each sport. This will help make your decision easier.

For instance, if you are cute and bouncy and have a ponytail (I'm not even talking about the women) and if your name ends in the letter "i," then volleyball may be for you. Personally, I couldn't commit to any sport that had me in a bathing suit all day long. After a certain age (and for me it was 8) I've learned never to bend over in front of anyone when my midriff is showing.

Now, biking has a lot to offer with those groovy Coolmax spandex shorts. Personally, I could do without the big wad of cotton in the seat. I know it can be a life saver on rugged terrain for you men, but it's literally overkill for us women unless you like wearing 11 Maxi pads. But the shoes that click on are a wonderful thing (except inside, when it sounds like a poodle walking on a hardwood floor) and you do get to eat all those foods in gel tubes with names like Propel and Rocket and Lift Off, like you're on some secret space mission.

Okay, if you like to spit and chew and scratch your crotch, then baseball is for you. And if you're very hairy, and/ or from a foreign country, and/ or like to dress like a bee, I'd go for soccer.

Running has two categories. The first is more like jogging. There are lots of outfits for that: mix-and-match sweats and headbands and water bottles. The second group (which includes me), will wear pretty much anything. In fact, it's not beneath me to wear a T-shirt on my head, since there is no ozone layer and I can now tan at 6 A.M.

Let's put it this way: sometimes I meet my boyfriend outside when I'm running and he pretends he never met me, which is really OK. I do the same to him, because the hat he wears when he walks the beach looks like a lampshade from 1950.

Here is just a smattering of other outfits and paraphernalia to help you decide what kind of exercise might be right for you. If you're into thigh-high rubber boots or like hanging weird stuff from your hat, there's fishing. There's golf...What can I say, it says it all. If you like helmets and pads, there's football and wrestling and boxing and fencing and skateboarding and blading and motorcycling and driving the freeway. You can wear anything while boating, so don't go spending your money on a great bathing suit only to put on a dirty orange vest that smells like New Jersey.

Tights, masks, flippers, all kinds of goggles—the list

is never ending. Still can't decide? Not feeling self-determined? Try the gym. Have you been to one lately? There's everything you can possibly want: you can get steamed, take a sauna, get massaged, waxed, even plucked. You can kick-box, body-pump, body-step, body-flow, take Pilates, yoga, spin, tan. Bring the kiddies, climb a wall!

There are now TV sets every six inches. You can learn to grout or check up on your stocks. Heck, in my gym, I can learn open-heart surgery and do my abs at the same time. Have you ever noticed how you pretend you're watching CNN when someone cute is around, but right before that, you were watching that "Brangelina" thing. It is also interesting that not one soul can resist watching Michael Jackson's face on TV. You don't want to, but you can't help it.

I do hope you find this information fun and useful. Exercise can only enhance the joy of fully living life. So pick something that delights you, and commit to it. The key is, keep your word.

Optional Assignment

Make a date with yourself. Get out your date book and schedule regular exercise time for the next three weeks. Keep the gradient low. The object is to get the win. I'll see you on the beach. (I'm the one in the tutu with the ski mask on my head).

ON MONEY

I was watching the Comedy Channel several months ago and there was this comic named Bill Hicks doing a very funny bit about linking sex with advertising and how it boosts sales. So while he was yelling out names of different products, he would hold these very erotic bendy sexual postures, reminding me of a cross between the Kama Sutra and those cheesy black-light astrological sex posters from the 60's.

You know, like Gemini, two upside-down women and a guy with an Afro (sounds like a TV show). Or Libra, bent over, heinie up (now Virgo I would understand, because they're always bending over straightening and cleaning stuff, but Libra?). And really, besides Gumby and girls named Nadia, who can get in those postures anyway?

So pretty much he's striking these poses, spreading his legs, and fake licking his imaginary bosoms like in "Girls Gone Wild, " yelling out products like Mr. Clean and Dr. Pepper. My personal favorite was his rendition of Snickers: bent at the waist, smiling and looking through his legs, which has now become a running joke between my boyfriend and I. "Hey Hon...*Snickers*" (gets him every time).

Anyway, my point is that the advertising industry, like most big businesses, wants us to believe that every human need can be satisfied by buying or obtaining something. You can get mates and dates through aftershave, lotions, deodorants, and mouthwash. You can get happy and have social skills through little pink and purple pills. Humiliation is banished if your panties are lined. Everybody knows you can stay confident through douching, have great friend-filled weekends from beer, and of course have wild sex for 18 hours with Viagra, and what working woman with six kids wouldn't want that!? All this to convince us that we are empty or inadequate; that we need something or someone or all sorts of items outside of ourselves to be whole and complete.

Is money bad? No. Is wanting and buying stuff bad? Of course not. Money is money. It's an exchange. It can be handy, useful, motivating--a tool. Like everything, it's all how we look at it and how we hold it. But what I'm talking about here is addiction. Looking outside of ourselves produces frenzy and fear, the opposite of freedom, health, self-esteem and wholeness, which doesn't cost a penny.

It's about choice and simplicity. Simplicity needn't be monk-like or self-denying. Some of us are wired to *not* pleasure ourselves or enjoy stuff, which is actually the other side of the same coin.

Here's a little example, which I learned three minutes ago. I've never been a big car person. So when my dented `95 Ford Aspire (they made two of them) started acting up, of course I went to fix it. But after months of one thing after another, the car was just plain losing it. Let's put it this way, in order to get the car up the hill you had to shut off the air, heater, and radio and push back and forth with your body. I'll just say this: when the four-block-long big rigs in the slow lane get annoyed and try to pass you, it's time for another car.

Now, like a lot of you, I'm thinking, "I don't have the money for this," so I set out to find an "affordable" car--

which, by the way, is ridiculous. Also, no one tells you it's going to be a full time job. You get obsessed, not only with swirling questions inside yourself, like should I buy new or used? Take out a loan? Steal it? You start looking at every freakin' car on the road, scrambling like the day before a haircut and you're looking at everyone's head. "How can he afford that?" "He must be rich." "He doesn't look rich." My boyfriend and I are now having endless meaningful conversations about Blue Books, Spoilers, and MPG's. It's insane.

Secretly, I always wanted a V.W. Bug, but it was "way out of my price range." So I "settled" for another car. Without giving away it's name, I'll just say that it rhymes with Buzuki, which literally ended up being called Puki, because every time I got into this thing, I thought I was gonna puke. This was not a new car smell. This was a brain frying, memory erasing, drool on yourself, Chernobyl-on-wheels, and personally I do want to keep the remaining brian (I mean, brain) cells I have left from the 60's.

I'm now paying monthly "affordable" payments on Smellen Keller and I can't even get in the thing, let alone to work. The Buzuki people are not helping, so now I'm renting a car. Everything I try to clean the car with makes it worse, and I have to start looking at cars all over again. Long story short: I end up with a used V.W. Bug and with the hit I took, I'm now paying more than if I bought it new, fully loaded and with enough left over to feed half of Pakistan. Besides seeing that I came from a place of scarcity, what else did I learn? Go for what you want. Really. Don't settle. After all, denial, like anorexia, is still an eating disorder.

There must be a trillion money books on the market-- "How to Get Rich and Screw Your Friends"; "How to Get Rich and Not Screw Your Friends"; and "How to Think and Grow Rich and Grow Hair at the Same Time"--most supporting our aberrant notions that we define ourselves by the things we can acquire, rather than seeing who we really are and what we really need to be able to live well, happy and fulfilled lives.

Take just one moment and ask yourself, Do you rule money or does money rule you?

Optional Assignment

How do you feel about how you spend your time? Do you enjoy the work that you do? Does it make you happy? Fulfilled? Connected? If your monthly nut was covered or better yet, if you had all the money in the world, what would your day look like? What would you do with your time?

Now write down the things you want to do and care most about. Is it really money that prevents us from the experience that we want, or is it our belief about money? I struggle with this myself, but it helps me to remember to make a life, not a living.

TO YOUR HEALTH

You know how you teach what you need to learn? Well, I notice I spend a lot of my time talking to patients and writing about how we look outside ourselves to fill or fix someplace inside. To be really honest, I do that, especially when it comes to my physical health. I am extremely disciplined, so it's not like I don't "do" what I know to be healthy: exercise, eat well, be of service, etc. But man-o-man, when I honestly look at myself, I have been going about "health" quite frantically, running to healers, health food stores, pouring through books, journals, taking classes, and workshops.

This is crazy. How do I know this? Let's put it this way, I just cut someone off on the road because I was late for my acupuncture appointment. Now, I'm not proud of this, but it is not beneath me to drive pretty much up someone's heinie to hurry them along so I can get home in time to meditate.

I've also been known to rudely hang up on telemarketers so I can get to my mantras and affirmations declaring that "WE ARE ALL ONE." This pursuit of healing is darn near killing me and apparently others as well. You get my point, stressing and pushing and running around to get fixed is insane. It's not only a statement that says, "right here, right now is *not* OK," but it also totally negates the healer within us.

125

Am I saying don't take action or seek help? No. If you're sick or hurting in some way, getting help can be just the ticket. But how do you go about it? Do you do it with ease and grace? Does it ultimately empower you and move you towards greater freedom and independence?

We've all heard stories about hospitals where a guy goes in to get a bunion removed and he comes out with a vasectomy and breast implants. Or when a woman goes in for a simple "procedure" and they take out her ovaries, uterus, tonsils, all her molars and 63 feet of her intestinal tract "just in case." Why don't they just answer the phone and call it like it is--"Hello, Roach Motel." Or, "Hello, Bermuda Triangle Medical Center."

Look who we're putting our trust in. Instead of handing over our power to others, call me crazy, but I think it's time to look within for our own physical, emotional, and spiritual well being.

Some months ago I took this wonderful workshop about Qi Gong (like Tai Chi) and healing. I took it for three reasons: 1. I needed the units to keep my license going. 2. I secretly hoped it might fix me and 3. I got to go away for six days. Now I don't want to come off like one of those people, who, when they find something that works for them, try to shove it down everyone's throat. But it woke me up to life energy and to self-healing.

Even though it's a new mindset for me and I know *bubkis*, I am clear about one thing: all this running around is depleting. It's addictive and possibly the very thing keeping some of us sick--not to mention dependent--and feeding a system that has nothing to do with real health and our own natural abilities to heal.

OK, how do we do this? The first thing is to accept. Accept ourselves and our bodies exactly where they are. That's right, pain, illness, fat, thin, whatever. Here

126

we are. Resistance creates more pain, and I never knew anybody who moved into a stable flourishing place of health through self-loathing and rejection. Secondly, illness, pain, etc., can be a teacher, a barometer. Are we around people or in situations that are holding us back? Are we looking to others for our sustenance and holding them responsible for our own self care and well being? Do we come from a place of self love? Is there balance?

It's all an opportunity to look at our lives, not only our physical habits, but our thoughts, ethics, and actions. There is no question that being sick can be a humbling experience, but like other challenges in life, it can also be transformative and ultimately empowering.

Optional Assignment

Want to change the world? Pick one thing each day to promote and enhance your health and well being. Take a breath, and get centered. We are all interrelated. If each one of us took better care of ourselves we would change the health care system. And maybe Kaiser wouldn't be so permanente.

ON STRESS

What is stress? Well, first there are things called "stressors," like traffic, a loud noise or neighbor, an asteroid heading toward earth. The range is enormous. So "stress" is the way our body reacts to these stressors.

A lot happens to our bodies when we get stressed. Just like the "fight or flight syndrome," where your body goes into high gear to prepare for a potential threat. Our bodies release adrenaline and nora drenaline (I went to high school with her) and prepares for action. All this increases blood pressure, blood sugar, cholesterol, and cortisol levels, as well as breathing and heart rate (there's a test after this, but you can use your books).

Not all stress is bad. It can really get us going, infusing us with energy and creativity. But long-lasting stress can be hard on us, to say the least.

Stress is inevitable. It's crazy out there. I actually got the finger in the parking lot at the health food store (is nothing sacred?). The key is how fluid we are in our ability to stay centered and handle all of life's stressors. So how do we do this? Well, to begin with, forget the quick fixes like smoking or drugs or alcohol or sex or Oreos. They will backfire, even if you think the cream in the Oreo contains traces of calcium and that it is a good way to prevent osteoporosis.

Try this. On a scale from 1-10, ten being stressed out, one being nirvana, where are you right now? Read this first, then close your eyes (not the other way around). Gently inhale through your nose and imagine the #4. Then exhale through your nose, letting go of the #4. Then inhale #3 (same thing). Exhale #3. Then do the same thing with #2, then #1. Really, try this. It will only take seconds. Now, take a read. Did your needle come down? Better or worse? (like the eye doctor). Take a read periodically throughout the day. Try and stay under a 6 if possible. If you are an 8 or 9 or 10, it won't take much for you to blow.

Now, if you're like me, "sponge girl" (or Bob, if you're a boy), and you walk around feeling other people's energy, there are options. One is to stay home. Never go out. I tried that once but I ran out of Chunky Monkey. I even tried putting crystals in my brassiere for protection, but personally, besides being too pointy, I also found it kinda scratchy. The other option is when you get home or at the end of the day, even if your day was a great one, take a good-bye shower. That's right. Get in the shower and say goodbye to everyone you've encountered, even the dog. Say goodbye and wash off everyone, one by one. "Bye Brittany," "Bye Justin," "Bye Elvis."

There are tons of ways to de-stress. Try using color. According to experts, pink lowers blood pressure and pulse rate, while red is arousing. Black lowers oxygen levels. Green may actually increase stress (hospital uniforms!). People in blue rooms describe themselves as calmer and happier than those tested in rooms with red, yellow, or neutral colors. Play with this.

Other ways to reduce stress is through music. In the book, "The Secret Life of Plants," a study was done where they experimented with different types of music and its effects on plants. They found that heavy metal and heavy rock music actually hurt the plants. Country music had no effect at all. When they played classical music, the plants flourished. When they played classical Indian music, the plants loved it so much that they wrapped their tendrils around the speakers. So next time you want to score, just put on "Love Songs from the Punjab: the Indira Gandhi Years."

There are literally thousands of ways to de-stress and not get arrested. Get a massage, take a bath, do yoga, exercise. Get into nature, biofeedback, or visualizations. Read, write, draw, kiss, dance, sing, sleep, let the sun warm your back--the list is endless. Look at how you spend your time and who you spend your time with. Do you feel empty? Depleted? Are you frantically running around? Do you feel motivated? Creative? Useful?

Look at the food you are eating. Someone once told me the key to staying healthy is to eat only foods from the outer aisles of a market: fruits, vegetables, seeds, nuts, fish. Never eat the stuff inside the aisles. For stress, the body needs to be balanced and hydrated.

Learn what your body really needs. Most importantly, take care of yourself first. Your reach will be bigger, and you'll have more to give.

Optional Assignment

Write down everything that delights you. Colors, smells, music, people, places, flowers, sensations-- anything. If you like to rub the belly of your dog, or wife, or neighbor, or your neighbor's wife, write it down. If you love the sound of leaves crunching under your feet in the fall, write it down. Get into it.

Now take this list. Unless it harms you or someone

131

else, jump into it. If you love berries, eat them, roll in them, whatever. If you love purple, wear it. Allow yourself to be fed. Engage all your senses. If you really want to contribute to the planet, de-stress. You just wrote out exactly what you can do. Now go do it.

PART IV.
OPENING YOUR HEART
TO LIFE

HOT HUMBLE PIE

Can you picture how great life could be if we didn't take it all so seriously? That instead of the stress of needing to look or be a certain way, we were light enough to just drop it and be fine both with our magnificence and, how should I say, "lack of magnificence."

You know those humbling moments in life when you think you're coming off really cool or profound or whatever and then you check yourself out in the mirror only to find you had something hanging out of your nose or enough lettuce in your teeth to make salad for six? That's me. That's my life. Heck, I once did an entire session with a rice cake on my head. Literally. Not just some crumbs stuck in my hair. No. An entire rice cake cracker perched on the top of my head.

I was sitting there thinking, "I'm on a roll. The session's going really well. My client's smiling--almost laughing." Good Lord! I didn't even know until she was long gone and I looked at my head! How did it even get there? Was I eating before the session, and the phone rang, so I stuck the cracker on my head to better answer the call, then I forgot about it? I still don't get it.

Anyway, truly, I am the Queen of Uncool. I have tons of these experiences. Every time I'm too full of myself or want to look a certain way or get way too serious, something always happens to lighten me up or humble me out.

This has been happening as far back as grade school when I came out of the bathroom with my dress up in the back. Thank God Jeffrey Cedarbaum threw up his milk that day and we had to go outside, lessening my full day of humiliation by one half.

When I was to meet my first boyfriend's mother for the first time I really wanted to impress her. It was a cool summer night. He came to pick me up. I grabbed a clean shirt right out of the dryer to warm me up. I didn't even realize until after dinner and I had excused myself from her table, that I had a wide assortment of designer panties and sweat socks statically clinging to the back of my shirt. Smooth, huh?

Then there was my first sexual experience. I had planned it very carefully. I went to Planned Parenthood, got my first diaphragm, and I was ready. That night when things started getting intimate, I excused myself from the room, went into the bathroom and re-read the directions for the 83rd time to be sure that I was doing it right. "Fill the disk with the jelly...squeeze the sides slightly together"...then this thing slides right out of my hand, pops up into the air, and suctions onto the ceiling! After my initial shock (I looked like a white Buckwheat from the Little Rascals), I could not stop laughing. I spent the rest of my evening trying to get it down with the back of a broom.

I once got fired from a job at a bakery for eating too much of the profits. On the humiliation scale from 1 to 10 where "1" is whatever and "10" is "I'm dying here," it was about a "15."

Not too long ago I was asked to give a talk at a home for battered women. I really gave it a lot of thought. I wanted to talk about repeating old patterns, the power of thoughts, moving into self-love, etc. The day before I was to give this talk I was in a mall and walked smack into a huge glass door and got the biggest black eye in recorded history. So the next day, there I was standing in front of these battered women with a big fat shiner--all black and blue. What am I gonna say? Is life great or what?

My boyfriend had a good one. He was giving a presentation of his photographs before his college class. He was up there feeling pretty good about himself telling jokes, with people laughing. They were smiling, he was smiling, everyone was smiling. He was thinking, "Hey, I'm pretty good at this. Yeah, they really like my work." The presentation ends with him discovering the real presentation. Not only is his zipper down but his pants are completely wide open with half of his underwear trying to escape. I love it! Apparently the crowd loved it too.

No matter how confident we feel, or how much planning we do, life sometimes has plans of its own. It's up to us how seriously we want to take ourselves or our circumstances. When it comes right down to it, what truly matters is how lightly we hold it all. The truth is that once we let go, we see that life is not only beautifully orchestrated, but can be really really funny. In closing, it's all about accepting our inner Moe, Larry and Curly.

Optional Assignment

The world has gotten way too heavy. Look around. Look at the news. We have forgotten the art of levity and divine silliness. It's time to change our perspective. To look and be in the world in a whole different way.

Do one thing today that you enjoy or makes you laugh:

- *Wave at people you don't know.*

- *Walk backwards.*

- *Wear a clown nose to your next AA meeting.*

- *Hang out with some 4 or 5 or 6 year olds.*

- *Paint some fruit on black velvet and display it proudly.*

Anything. Take a risk. You've got nothing to lose, except maybe your seriousness.

WAKE UP ON AISLE NINE!

You ever see the movie, "Night of the Living Dead", where all these zombies are walking around, pointing their fingers and making weird sounds when they open their mouths? Well, that's what it's like at my neighborhood SuperStore.

No really, I was there the other day looking to buy a cell phone. So I walk in and go over to this guy whose badge says, "Mort" (how could I know at the time, it was short for riga-Mort-us?), and ask where the electronic department is. He gives me that vacant "Children of the Damned" kind of look and procedes to point east...then west...then down, which I'm thinking may not be such a good sign.

Anyway, there I am, a first time shopper, going up and down the aisles. I cannot believe the selection at this place. You can buy anything! Where else can you buy a TV and a cheese wheel all under one roof? My favorite, though, at the checkout counter right near the Chia Pets and The Clapper, is a bunk bed. Like it's an impulse item or something. "Oh yeah, a bunk bed...I forgot!"

At any rate, I spotted the electronic department (which, by the way, is between home perms and swim-ming pools) and found the telephones, which of course were all locked up. Fine jewelry I could understand, but an $18.95 Go Phone?

So after ten minutes of approaching pretty much everyone--"Do you work here?"..."Do YOU work here?"--I finally found some teenager to help me. He was completely plugged into his iTune-iPod thing. I could actually hear the music coming through his head. So could aisle 9, for that matter. I kind of figured that if I followed him, he would spring the phone I wanted.

This kid did not look at me or say one word. He did grunt, though, but maybe he was singing or had some gas. I don't know. But life has a sweet way of working out. Plus, I didn't have the heart to tell him that when he grows up, it'll be humiliation enough when he looks back at pictures of himself with the crotch of his pants below his knees.

As I'm walking towards the front to pay for my item, I'm noticing this place is filled with the "undead." Truly, people walking around, stocking shelves, pushing carts-- expressionless. The only thing missing is Michael Jackson singing "Thriller" over the loudspeaker.

I'm thinking, "What the heck's going on here? Are they passing out free samples of Valium in the feminine hygiene and cramps section?" (Which, by the way, is across the aisle from toilet seats and next to the frozen meat.) Where's the life? The energy? The joy? My whole body started to spin.

Then, I spotted her: Angelika, 12-items-or-less. She was amazing, and the blood to my head and my faith in the human race started to return. She was perfection. Real "Guinness Book" stuff. Her customers were bagged and out the door before they knew what hit them. Her stats were incredible. A work of art. I counted. She was doing six customers to everyone else's one, all the while smiling, like an angel.

So what's the difference between Angelika and the attitude of Mr. i-"Pod"?. They're both doing the same job. Why does doing the same work produce different responses? Well, one person is fully in the moment, living it, joyfully servicing others. There's no duality or duplicity. Nothing stands between Angelika and her customers. The "Pod People," on the other hand, seem to be immersed in their own thinking and resistance. Undoubtedly, they don't want to be there in the first place. They are "dead" to their world.

As I see it, if you've outgrown or hate what you are doing, give yourself permission to get out. Seek to do the thing that engages you and makes your life worthwhile. If you're in a situation that you cannot move on from right now, treat it and yourself, with loving kindness. Always. This is your life. Stay conscious. Stay open. If you do, the gifts may surprise you.

The bottom line is this: It's not what we "do" that makes us or our life, it's the *life* in what we do that makes us who we are.

Optional Assignment

Look at your own life. How are you showing up? Involved? Interested? Open? Present? Write down what you could do to make your world richer, fuller, more expansive and fun. Pick one thing off your list and do it. Is there really anything or anyone stopping you? Why not make the most of each moment.

GIVING

This really sweet woman came to see me several years ago. She said she was new to the city and that she felt isolated, sad, and really alone. So I could quickly get to know her better, I asked her to bring in pictures, books, music, bagels, chocolate (the last two items were for me) that would tell me more about who she was. For instance, if she's a runner, she might bring in sneakers. If she watches a lot of TV, the remote…anything she could think of that could tell me about her life and her world.

So at our next meeting, she comes in with bags filled with all sorts of stuff and as she starts spreading it all over the floor, I'm noticing there's a theme in every item she lays out. In every photo there's people close together, hugging or holding each other. There is tons of little love objects that people had given her along the way. There's pictures of pets, of nature, of kids she's sponsored and helped-- pictures of children all over the world that, as she put it, "have graced my heart." I'm thinking, "This woman is one big loveball."

Of course, she's sad and in pain.

Being disconnected and alone is not her natural state. Her heart was all dressed up with nowhere to go. Loving and connecting gave this woman meaning and purpose. Giving was her bliss.

When you're new, it's hard to have an "instant" best

friend or partner or family. Wouldn't it be cool if you could just type in on your computer the kind of family or partner you want. Input a little sample of your DNA (I always have a little extra in case there's company), slide in your Visa or Discover Card and voila, in just 6 to 8 business days, you're set. Instant loved ones! I can just picture the malfunctions in the beginning while they're working out the kinks. "I wrote Cleaver, not Beaver" (or for some of you, just the opposite), "I wrote Blonde, not Blind", or "Jew, not Blue..."

Anyway, the two of us got busy and came up with a plan to get her heart flowing again. The form didn't matter. She didn't have to cure cancer or go around finding blind people to walk across the street. She decided she would simply do one thing each day that made it better for someone or something. In a matter of days, this woman felt a greater happiness within. Just simple acts of expressing love or kindness or compassion actually caused her to feel more connected and more alive.

Through this woman I began to see that most of the people that I work with were experiencing the same thing. I saw that there is really no "pathology" or "sickness." It's only that we sometimes forget we are all connected, and that giving and flowing love not only keeps us healthy, but is an integral part of why we are here.

Now, there are all kinds of giving. There's giving to get something back (I used to give Bazooka gum to my entire second grade class so they'd like me--it totally worked). Some of us give because we feel we are not enough, so we need to do something to get the love of others. Some of us give because we think we should (like when the collection plate is passed around).

There's over-giving where the exchange between two people is unbalanced. Both people usually end up feeling

144

pretty badly, resentful or indebted. There's giving that really feels good--a donation or contribution--usually with some kind of reward, like a pat on the back or a tax deduction. Then there's giving to benefit others without, not because of, the expectation of some kind of payback or reward. I guess that's called true altruism (sounds like a guy's name doesn't it? Al Truism, he's my accountant).

So why does giving feel so good? Some scientists say that we are "hardwired" for giving. That generosity feels good because a rush of dopamine is released in the brain when we do. It's pleasure producing. Others say goodness resides in every one of us and that love and compassion is our true nature. That we all carry within us an urge or yearning for some kind of union or oneness. In other words, we long to be one not only with ourselves but with each other. Giving brings us together.

There are thousands of things that people do every day from the goodness of their hearts that go unnoticed. People *are* pretty great. It's all how you look at it.

Optional Assignment

Start now. Just decide.

Give thanks, compliments, time, compassion, anything you'd like. Put money in someone's meter. Make or buy food and give it out. Put clothes or blankets in the back of your car for people who might need them.

Simplify, listen to one another, tell jokes, accept each other, give to yourself. We are all parts of the whole. We are all blessed with something to give. Find it and flow your gift.

ON CONTRIBUTION

Years ago, I took an undergraduate class on world events. The truth is, I took this class because I heard there were no formal tests and that the teacher was hip, cute, and didn't give homework. By the way, why is it that when you go to school for psychology, the instructors either look like Moses, Santa Claus, or Eleanor Roosevelt? To say the least, between the penis envy and Oedipus Rex, this class was a welcome change. The only requirement for this course was that we were to do something on the planet that we felt might make a difference, find some form of contribution.

In those days, I was a fashion illustrator. Yes, I confess. I would draw non-ethnic anorexic men and women all day long (only to go home to 18 gallons of Cherry Garcia at night). It felt really warm inside to know that I was a part of perpetuating the myth that we should all be white and weigh 102.

I'm surprised I wasn't on heroin.

Anyway, for my project, I figured out a way to get clothing to the homeless and infirm. Not just clothing, but designer clothing. So pretty much there were these people living in boxes or some sprawled out in their own urine, throwing up in their Yves Saint Laurent reptile skin boots, with DKNY or Jordache embroidered on their behinds.

At the end of the class, we were supposed to stand up

and tell everyone what we had done during the semester. It was interesting. There I was, feeling kind of good about myself because I had done this wonderful thing. One person worked with the elderly, another with prisoners, and still another with failing babies. Some were saving our oceans. Some were saving our trees--you name it. We were all pretty impressed with ourselves.

Then this lady stood up and said, "I stopped speeding on the Freeways." I'm thinking, "How lame. Stopped Speeding?" Then she said, "Oh, I'm gonna continue to do this even when the class is over." The truth was I couldn't wait for the class to be over. It was a pain in the butt to keep it all going. It then dawned on me. I went for the flash, what sounded good. "I give clothes to the home-less"--impressive, huh? It really appealed to my ego. What this woman taught me was that it's the quiet, con-sistent things that matter. Now that's powerful: simple, mindful contribution.

So far, from what I can see, we all have three basic needs: to be loved, to give love, and to do something meaningful. I think we are all running around trying to get these needs met. Clearly, it can get pretty wild.

First, the love thing. Look around. You can see people turning themselves inside out and upside down in order to be loved. Maybe if I was skinny enough, young enough, rich enough, smart enough, then they'd love me. We stay in all kinds of relationships looking for that Cos-mic Love Feeling, where our whole being can fully exhale and just be. Again, the ability to experience love lies in accepting and loving ourselves, as well as marveling at all the beauty and magic that resides in each other. When we come from this place, flowing love is a natural.

We all seek meaning or purpose or a reason to put our shoes on in the morning. If you want to feel useful, purposeful, and a part of all things, being of service just may be the ticket. Again, it's not about curing Aids or rickets (do they still have that?) or scurvy (which I think is a pirate thing) or even in the doing. It's more about our state of being. It's simple. Be clear and be present and come from love. We all have a huge ripple effect. Everything we do or don't do or think makes a difference. Everything and everyone is connected. It's the stuff under the radar that appears insignificant that is the most transformative.

One person doing one thing seems like nothing. But times that by six billion people or even a fraction of that and you've got a revolution!

Optional Assignment

Can't figure out how to contribute? Here are some more ideas: slow your mind, blow your mind. Have more fun. Cultivate joy. Stop shopping, except for food. Use the library. Change your routine, or your lightbulbs. Shake it up. Drive less, walk more. Let someone in line before you. Recycle. Let ants live. Dance more. Sing more. Create more. Love more. Learn more. And definitely, definitely laugh more. Pick something and try it. Remember: You really start living when you really start giving.

WHAT'S RIGHT

That's it. I've so had it with the news. First of all, I don't care what station you're watching these days--Fox, CNN, the BBC, or whether it's in Spanish, Chinese, Arabic, Yiddish ("Oy, you wouldn't believe the tumult in Beirut! I'm just plotzing"), or how hip or cute or perky or jiggly the newscaster is--the news is evil. There, I've said it.

Try this: Iran, Iraq, Korea, Kabul, Tehran, and Kuwait... What do all these have in common? Besides cheap airfare, their very names conjure up bad associations. They make us feel awful, unless of course you think the Golan Heights is in Brooklyn, the West Bank is in France, and the Gaza Strip is in Vegas.

Now also try this: Heavenly, California; Love Field, Texas; St. Cloud, Minnesota; or Philadelphia, Pennsylvania... Besides the city of brotherly love, they've also got the cream cheese. Unless you've gotten hit by a meteor in any of these places, these names bring up feelings of pleasure--don't they? Would you rather live in Sugarland, Texas, or Waco? Darlington, South Carolina or Deadwood? Mount Pleasant, Michigan or Battle Creek? You get my point.

Now take words like "suicide bomber," "Al Qaeda," "tsunami," "Richter Scale," and link them to the visuals: piles of debris and dead bodies, flood footage usually taken from old Hollywood disaster movies, and bango! It's locked into our consciousness. No wonder we're living on Prozac and Twinkies.

I can just see it now, a whole new line of products: *Overwhelmed? In a Hurry?* Now you can combine both food *and* drugs, like *Heroin Helper, Pot Tarts, Ritalin N' Rice, Cup O' Ludeles, Smackeroni and Cheese, Spaghetti and Goofballs*, and of course for those on the go, handy, hearty and wholesome, *Paxil Pudding Pops*!

So you're watching the news lying on your bed or couch, and just when you think you can't take it any more, they throw in that cute little otter or panda story from the zoo. Little Ling-Ling (you notice they never name them after Jewish accountants, like Murray or Herschel) sucking on a bottle, and everyone coos and smiles and gets all giggly. That's usually when I start craving a Lithium Latte or a McHighball.

Am I saying that bad things don't happen or that we should deny its existence? Of course not, but there are zillions of things that go right everyday: so many miracles and contributions and blessings and funny stuff. Why is *that* not on my TV or in my cable package? Where's the balance?

Are catastrophes more interesting than stories of inspiration or creativity? I don't think so. We're just lulled and numb and used to looking at what's wrong. We're not taught to focus on or value what's right.

Most couples who first come to me are so fixed on looking at what is wrong with each other: "She's glued to the phone."; "He never comes home."; "She flirts with her ex"; "He always wants sex." If we could come to our relationships more fed and centered, we would be able to experience and acknowledge what is right.

I'm not talking about being happy all the time. I'm talking about appreciation and gratitude, about opening our-selves up to wonder and amazement. I'm talking about seeing the world with different eyes. Eyes filled with goodness, compassion, and grace. To see through these eyes is to know that ultimately everything has its place and that everything is really all right.

Optional Assignment

For one day, write down the many things that go right for you. Start to train yourself to notice all the wonders around you. Use your senses. Feel the wind on your face. Go into a bakery and take a whiff. Look up at the sky. Time to regroup. Shut off your TV's and unplug from the media and newspapers and magazines. Let yourself have this experience. It just might change your life.

KARMA

Did you ever have "one of those days"? Early this morning I set out to do some errands. Simple enough. So I go to the car. Flat tire. OK, it happens. I've got AAA. So I call and I wait. I wouldn't say I waited very long, but let's put it this way, I read the entire V.W. manual, cleaned out the glove compartment and trunk, chewed 11 packs of gum, flossed, gave myself a manicure, returned all my phone calls (I now have a dental appointment next Monday and a gyno exam Thursday at 2:45), sang to the entire Beatles "White Album," and just when I was about to give myself a sponge bath, Goober came. Really, that was his name.

OK, day off--no hurrying. So I have 212 things to do. Now Goober can't find where to stick his jack, so he starts muttering something about how tight lug nuts can be (which I'm sure can be quite painful), and keeps calling me Mrs. Paul. Mrs. Paul?! I'm not a fish stick and just give me a clue, where did he get Mrs. Paul? OK, finally Goober slaps on my spare, which is the size of a Scooter Pie, and off I go to get the tire fixed.

Wait. It goes down from there. Starting with Moe, Larry, and Shemp at the tire store, who can't repair the tire (I must admit it had a hole in it the size of a regulation basketball), there are also several cars ahead of me and I am # 26.

155

OK, OK, BREATHE, I tell myself. Just go with it. So I decide to wait in the room with the motor oil and nude car magazines and watch daytime TV, which I haven't seen since I was home sick from school. So I watched the same "Lucy" episode from 1963 (you know, the one with William Holden), some of "Montel," and around the time "People's Court" started getting really good, my car was ready.

I will spare you the rest of the day, but let's put it this way, after the bank with the one teller, the postal worker who was the slowest person I ever saw and had to be on some kind of combination Lithium and Demerol, and the hot broccoli garlic soup spilling out of the earth-friendly biodegradable container pretty much all over the trunk of my car, I came home to find that the lens on my headlight had popped off (apparently the previous owner thought it would be wise to seal it with Silly Putty) and that I had run over it when I rushed out to meet Goober.

After I finally got home and bolted the door, I got to thinking, which was not easy since someone tripped the house alarm in the building across the street and I think the guy who lives there is in Cuba or something and won't be home for another dos weeks. As I was recapping my day, I was looking at "What's up here"? Now I do tend to blame myself for most everything--global warming... that's me; famine...me too. But I do believe that what goes around comes around in some form or another. Was it karma? (Or "car-ma"?) Is there really such a thing? Did I rape a nun last time? Was it just a bad day? What?

Now we all have bad days, and I don't know if having a trunk that smells like the limburger cheese section of some deli is karmic, but I do notice that there are certain laws of cause and effect, that when most people harm others, they end up feeling really badly and ultimately tend to get caught, self-punish, or self destruct. Now is

156

this because most of us are basically good? Is it karma?

The notion of karma appeals to me in that it deals with ethics and intention, which requires a certain kind of mindfulness. It implies that we are interrelated and that our past creates the present, and that we all have the capacity at every moment to change the future.

Worse comes to worse, even if there is no such thing as karma, at least we've taken responsibility for ourselves and our planet.

Optional Assignment

Do something kind or loving today. It really does go a long way.

HALF FULL?

Here is a wonderful example of optimism. I go to this great neighborhood gym. It's unpretentious, warm, and friendly. Most of us are at least 40 and up (some way up). Though sometimes they play hip-hop and rap, like 50-cent and Justin Timberlake, in hopes of getting a younger crowd, half the gym just shuts off their hearing devices. Let's put it this way, if they play anything before 1966, the place literally goes wild.

Nobody loses weight at this gym. I actually saw a lady on the stair-master eating what looked to me like a meatball sub.

Anyway, I'm sitting next to this older gentleman on a bike the other day. I'm thinking he's in his mid-to-late 80's. I can usually tell a person's age by how long it takes to get on and off the exercise equipment. This guy took about an hour and 45 minutes to get on this thing. So we get to talking. He's terrific. He has one of those faces with twinkling eyes and lots of laugh lines. He starts talking about how he needed to replace the roof of his house--all the prices and choices he had to make, etc. Then he looks at me and says, "I went for the one with the 30-year warranty." Now, that's optimism.

OK, what is optimism? It is simply the belief that life is good. More good than bad, and that things will work out in the end. Or maybe it's just reacting to life in a positive manner. Pessimism? Well, it's from the Latin word "pe-simmus," which means "worst." That pretty much says it all. It's a belief that things are more bad than good, and probably won't work out in the end. Again, it's reacting to life in a negative manner.

There are all sorts of studies on what determines our nature. Some say we are all born optimistic, but it is what we are subjected to that changes our outlook. If we hear, "Life is hard," "Don't trust," "You can't..." and we see and experience it all around us, we begin to believe it and adopt a view of life that reflects that.

Conversely, if we hear, "Life is good" or "Safe" and "Go for it!" Well, this thinking also becomes our world view and a self-fulfilling prophecy. If indeed this is the case—that it's learned from the get-go—then this is very good news, because new things can always be learned, and with enough consciousness, we can choose the way we think about and experience life.

Let's look at how our thinking reinforces the state we're in.

I have this client. He's well educated, a pilot, lawyer, handsome, healthy, wealthy...and miserable. Why? Because he's always looking for what's wrong. No matter what he is blessed with, he views his life as forever doomed and empty. "His" world, like "the" world, is filled with wonderful things but he has trained himself to see the negatives in life. As a result, he is perpetuating an already hopeless state.

I've got this other client who, let's put it this way, if it were 1936, he would probably pay me in chickens or jam or some kind of live stock. He barely makes ends meet. He comes to therapy with jumper cables (jump-starting his car has now become part of our sessions). He is certain he will always have enough and make it to anywhere he needs to go. This guy is deeply rich because he is always looking at the treasures and blessings in what he does have.

As I see it, the world is pretty much indifferent. It's neutral. What is, is. We are the ones who assign all kinds of value to it--good, bad, right, wrong, urgent, not so urgent, scary, not so scary. Of the two—optimist and pessimist—who do you think lives a more joyful life?

Here's a quick story. This couple has two sons. One's an optimist; the other, a pessimist. They decide to test if they can influence or shift their son's natures in any way. So they give the pessimist son everything. They load him with all sorts of gifts and goodies. Everything they can imagine. But no matter what he gets, the son is still not satisfied. Then they decide to give the optimistic son one thing. A pile of horse poop. Yep. That's it. And as they're waiting for their son's reaction, the son smiles and exclaims, "There must be a pony around here somewhere!"

Optional Assignment

Write down all the events that have taken place so far today. For example, "I got up early," "I spilled my coffee," "I flirted at the gas station," etc. Take your emotions and put them to the side as you write. Now take that list and next to each item write down what's negative about it. Then take the same list and do it again, this time writing down what's positive. Same events, different mindset. You always have a choice.

PSYCHIC PHENOMENA?

*"There is no question that there is an unseen world. The problem is, how far is it from midtown and how late is it open?" - **Woody Allen, "Without Feathers"***

I had this amazing, lovely, smart, and very gifted client that came to me for a short while. She told me that when she was younger she had these natural psychic abilities, like reading people's thoughts and moving tiny objects, which I think would be incredibly handy, especially when you're feeling lazy and don't feel like getting something. You could just ask her to float over the salt or the remote, but apparently her mother wasn't of the same mind.

Anyway, seeing the upset she caused her family, she decided rather than nurture this gift, she'd do best to try and shut it down. Still in her "shut down" state, this woman was a powerhouse. I also have a friend like this who is tapped in and psychic. You can't ever lie to these people. You're so busted if you do. ("There were 20 people there." "How many?" "OK, 15." "How many?" "…Five").

Long story short, I had an emergency one day which conflicted with our appointment time and I tried and tried reaching her--cell phone, home phone, voice mail--I couldn't even get through to a machine. Nothing.

By the way, you notice everyone's got 48 numbers these days? I can no longer make friends with people whose last name starts with "S," because I have no more room in my phone book. I barely have room for one more "B" and possibly two more "P"s, unless I drop either my parents or the 11 pizza places in the immediate area.

Anyway, I decided, "Let's see how psychic this girl really is." So I start chanting, "Come at 3, not 5", "Come at 3, not 5." So 3 o' clock rolls around. She comes walking into my office, "Got your message, which worked out better for me." She is smiling a big smile. I am loving it. How do you explain this?

Here's another good one. I love to run. When I was younger I used to race quite a bit. As the years roll on, my racing is saved for those birthdays that end in zero or five. I guess to see if I've still got it. Last time zero came around it was time. Now, I like to think of myself as being in good shape, but at this stage of the game and in terms of racing, I'm probably somewhere in between the barefoot people from Kenya and the full term pregnant woman and the wheel chair guy.

I told my friend (the psychic guy mentioned above) that I was racing. Everyone's gonna want his number after I tell you this. He said he would pray for me which I thought was sweet but I really paid no mind to it. Day of the race comes: "On your mark. Get set. Go!" I take off. We're all running against the wind, and I'm struggling but giving it my best shot. All of a sudden--I swear I am not on crack--I felt like I was being lifted. I felt the presence of something on each side of me just effortlessly lift me up. I couldn't believe it. It was like I was gliding.

Because I have so much more to tell you, I'll make this story short. I won the race. How do I put this: I was not alone out there. So of course I immediately called my friend who prayed for me. He had the same smile in his voice that "psychic girl" had. Of course, now I want him to pray for me for everything—health, wealth, a new car, washer-dryer.... He just smiles.

I've got tons of these. Here's one along the same lines. My boyfriend's Mom was walking and lost her footing. She was about to fall slam onto the ground, but instead she was completely and gently lifted back up to her original standing position. Now this is not a woman who imagined it. This lady is pragmatic, sharp, vital, and not given to fantasy or an excessive imagination. This experience not only expanded her beliefs and deepened her sense of spirituality, but literally changed her life.

OK, here's one more. I once went to India. We were scheduled to go to the Taj Mahal but got delayed a few days. I couldn't believe the emotional reaction I had to this. I was completely distraught. Now you don't know me, but I don't easily get upset. So it was strange. Days later when we finally got there, again, I was overcome with deep emotion. I was overwhelmed with unexplainable joy. I started telling the people I was with all about the place. Not just the usual stuff. No. I knew everything down to the tile work in the back of the place. I knew the layout and all the colors. I knew the place like Opie knows Mayberry.

How do you explain this? Deja vu? Did I dip into the collective unconscious? Did I live there once before? I'm not saying I was the woman the place was built for. For all I know, I was Sabu the servant boy and knew the tiles so well because I was the person cleaning them. By the way, you ever notice when you talk about past lives everyone thinks they were someone special--a King or a Queen. I know like 12 Prince Valiants and 8 Cleopatras...

Anyway, here's my point. There is so much more that exists both within and outside our individual realities. Think of all the stuff that happens to us each and every day. The phone rings and you just know who it is or you're driving along and you just know who will change lanes and when. Can't you just sense the vibes off some people. Look at the connections between twins and lovers and mothers and fathers and children. You get my point. It's not about religion or belief or whether you think everything was created by a Supreme Being or some Cosmic Big Bang Energy or Force, but there's something divine within us, something that's universal that we can all connect to. How beautiful and fantastic is that?

Optional Assignment

Take a walk. Take someone you know and go for a walk. Now, blindfold them. That's right, blindfold them and gently lead them so they can begin to touch things and smell things, and without the use of sight, open up their other senses. You'll be amazed at what you'll discover. Sometimes we have to shut our eyes to really see.

NO PINS, NO PADS, NO BELTS

There are so many perks to my job. First, I get to help. I'm also privy to, and tapped into, the human condition which renders me extremely grateful and fills me with deep appreciation. Through my clients, I also get the latest in fashion and jargon and news from the outside world. They keep me current and informed. Without them, I'm thinking Gwyneth is still with Brad.

Another perk is that I can secretly gather information by listening to people's experiences. Not only does it broaden and enable me to help others better, but sometimes, I confess, it's for purely selfish reasons. Lately my own focus and quest for knowledge has been in regards to menopause, so I covertly, and I think artfully, try and weave the topic into most every conversation. "Oh, your mother likes green? Did that change for her after menopause?", or "You went rafting this summer? Did you need lubrication?" God, please forgive me.

Anyway, I'm noticing so many changes within myself--subtle ones, not just the obvious--and I'm wondering, "Is it just me or is it hot in here?" For example, I've now turned into that creepy old complaining woman at the gym. It literally happened overnight. This does not fill me with great pride to say this but all of a sudden, everything became too loud . . . and too windy and too smelly and . . . is this hormonal? Is this aging? I'm copping attitudes left

167

and right which I'm sure does wonders for my level of stress. My senses have become so acute that not only is perfume wigging me out, but I even know what everyone on the treadmill had for dinner the night before. "Oh, he had the braised sirloin tips with the broasted potatoes with just a hint of marjoram and thyme . . ." Oh, boy. Today I was next to garlic man and weird perfume girl, a cross between vanilla, musk and trout.

One more thing about the gym. I need to get this off my chest. I've been stuffing the suggestion box complaining about the music. I've been disguising my hand writing and using different names so they think its many people. "Please turn the music down. Thank you so much" - Helen Keller. Or, "I love your gym but the music sucks" – Abe Lincoln. Sometimes I like to use dead people's names so I don't get anyone in trouble. Back to menopause. So I'm researching like crazy and listening closely to my clients and friends about what goes on, or went on, for them through this process. This is what I've either experienced or gathered so far.

OK, you got your perimenopause which can last up to 10 years. You're still menstruating but now either every 86 days or every 3. Sometimes with the kind of cramps you had when you were 12 or if you just ate a whole bunch of bad pork. But every woman is different. Some of us have no symptoms whatsoever, while others may experience dryness, mood swings, insomnia, fatigue to name a few (sounds like the side effects for some acid reflux pill).

Then you got your menopause. This time, no periods. Again, some women just glide through this process and some really don't. By the way, if you haven't had a hot flash, let me give you an example so you can relate. You know those steamy saunas they have in Sweden, or the ones they used to have when Jack LaLane was about 20, where you can't breathe and see two inches in front of you? OK, pretend you just ate a jar of Jalapeño peppers, put on a snow suit like the kind they have in the Yukon, and took a handful of niacin. Got that? OK. Now get into the sauna. There you go.

And it comes on so suddenly. You'll innocently be talking about fish or something and within a nanosecond, BAM!, sweat's dripping off you fast and furiously and when it's over, your hair is completely matted, your eye make-up is now in your lap and your shirt looks like you just played a game of soccer.

I have these two clients, both going through the process of menopause with very similar symptoms. What's interesting is how differently these women are handling the changes in their bodies. "Attila" is pissed and dry and fighting it every step of the way. "Grace" is ecstatic, "no more pills and gels, no more cramping, bloating and frenzied eating." Same process, both have symptoms, but one is running from doctor to doctor looking for a pill to get out of her situation while the other--hot flashes and all--is discovering and learning to honor her new phase of life.

There are so many ways to handle this passage, both physically and emotionally. Whether you go the traditional route (hormone replacement therapy), or choose a more natural and biocompatible alternative (like yam cream, or anything on your Thanksgiving table for that matter) or a combo plate or nothing at all, may I make a suggestion? Don't let doctors or anyone scare you into anything because there is nothing to fear. It's another transition. You've been through many of them before. God willing, we will all go through this transition at some point in our lives. Make it graceful. Use it as an opportunity to get into a more loving relationship with yourself and all that you touch. Remember, in every life moment there is a present. Treasure it.

Optional Assignment

Whatever phase or cycle you may find yourself in, instead of trying to be somewhere you're not (like saying, "I'm too old" or "too young"), write down the gifts that are inherent in the stage you're at. Look for positives and what it brings to you, rather than the negatives. The best advice I could ever give you…It's always how you hold it.

ON FOOD AND AGING

Flashback: I'm 17, maybe 18 years old. I no longer live with my parents, but I'm still at the age where every once in a while I need to go home. With all the "Be Here Now" and "Let It Be's", I need a hit. I need a familial, primal, pot roasty, chicken soupy, 1950-ish, spaghetti-o kind of feeling. So I come home, saying my parents need to see me. Lots of changing trains - Grand Central and Penn Station. Finally, I'm there. Yes!

The house looks great, only smaller. Big hugs and kisses. And then at last, I go to that big Westinghouse altar (there should be religious background music for this). I open it. I can't believe what I see: V-8 juice with no salt. Metrical, remember that? Low fat this, nonfat that. Diet mayo. What the...? Where's my past? These are not my parents.

I check the cabinets. Not a Hostess Cupcake, Sno-Ball or Ding Dong. Not a nothing. Just low-salt tuna, no sodium soup. cling peaches with no sugar. What's the deal? I am confused. I check the address on the door. And then...it hits me, about the body and aging and heartburn and how life is so cruel.

Here I am, in my 50's. Having eaten at least 84 pounds of Fig Newtons alone. I have Fox's U-Bet chocolate syrup coursing through my veins. I even wear a Chips Ahoy cookie on my arm, just like the patch, to get through the day. I am sure that when I die and they open me up, they'll find either a fluffy creme filling or a soft nougat center. But here I am.

I went from Miss Fudgical to a health food freak, where everything is organic and on a bed of lettuce - to now - where even the bed of lettuce repeats on me and I now have to steam all of my vegetables just like my pants.

One last thing. Why is it that we all love to talk about food? What we ate? What we're gonna eat? What is our fascination to it? I guess food is love. It sustains us. It connects us. At this age when they say food binds us, I now literally know what they're talking about.

Optional Assignment

How many of us eat standing in front of the refrigerator? Or, how many of us eat standing over the counter or over the sink? (I have a friend who says they should have a singles restaurant where you can walk in and eat standing over a sink with your coat on). For one week, eat all your foods sitting down. See if you can pull this off. It's a truly nourishing thing to do.

RIP VAN WRINKLE

Don't go to sleep. Trust me, you really want to listen here. After a certain age...*don't* go to sleep. You know those wrinkles you get on your face from just lying on the pillow, just lying there? Sometimes you have your partner's whole entire hand print or a designer label imprint on your face, just like silly putty. The older you get, the longer it takes for those lines to go away. Truly, you can actually tell how old a person is by what time these lines disappear. It's more accurate than the rings of a tree. Let me say this, I normally don't leave the house till at least 4 or 5 p.m. these days.

And what's with that one long hair that just springs out of your neck or upper lip if you're a woman, that's about three-feet long and has the texture of 26-gauge steel wire? Now this is really weird because you didn't have it when you went to sleep for the final time after you dozed on and off through an entire Fred Astaire movie on TCM. (Ever notice that you nod off just right after Ginger or Cyd or Rita goes off to marry the guy with the pencil-thin moustache and you wake up exactly at the very end when she's back with Fred?). Okay, I know at this stage my eyes are shot and probably wouldn't spot a Zeppelin in the bedroom, but that hair, I don't think so.

Then there's the puffiness. I could dedicate a whole book to the mysteries of puffiness, but for now let's just say this--and this is also another very good reason to never go to sleep--massive, massive amounts of water can pop up literally *anywhere*: fingers, hands, feet, ankles, knees, one leg, yes, even one leg.

Seriously, one eye could be completely shut (the Popeye Syndrome), or both eyes (the Mister Magoo). Now this is not the same type of water retention you had before, during (and for some of us, after) menstruation. No, no. This is the kind that looks like the last stages of alcoholism, *before* the family intervention. And unlike the pillow wrinkles which disappear by early evening, this can go on for days or even weeks. I once looked like Robert DeNiro in "Raging Bull" for the entire month of December!

And here's another good reason not to go to sleep. Instead of getting up 4-5-7 times a night to urinate the quarter cup of water you had at 4:30 the day before, you can now spend the entire night in the bathroom. That's right, get used to it. But the good news is you can now catch up on all those back issues of "Greenpeace" and "The Sharper Image Catalogue."

Oh, and don't forget to keep plenty of reading glasses on and around the sink because you probably won't find the ones sitting on top of your head until you shampoo the next day and it comes out in the rinse cycle. So let out all the stops! Learn Latin, Kung Fu, How to Cook With Sateen. Heck, I even got my Ph.D. in there. Trust me...stay up. You'll thank me in the morning.

Optional Assignment

Every day for one week, list five things that's right about you. Each day make them different than the day before. Allow yourself to look deeply.

Allow yourself to see how wonderful you are.

Be aware of all the negative things you say to yourself throughout the day. Don't beat yourself up for beating yourself up. Just separate from it and counter with, "Thank you for sharing," or "I don't do that this week." Anything. In its place, start substituting what's right about you or the other person or the situation.

Remember, each thought has a chemical to it. And…

Always, always, go for the love.

Susan Pomeranz is a Marriage and Family Therapist who loves her work.

In addition to her private practice, she leads seminars and workshops throughout California. She has been a guest teacher at Antioch L.A., was featured on the radio, and has been a contributing writer for the "Ojai and Ventura Voice," where it's been reported that her hilarious columns have caused many a reader to eject food out of their nostrils (caution: please don't read them over a white carpet or after a heavy meal).

She lives happily in Southern California with her boyfriend, Norman.

CPSIA information can be obtained
at www.ICGtesting.com
Printed in the USA
LVHW111542030721
691839LV00003B/249